beetle bailey®

YOU CRACK ME UP

by mort walker

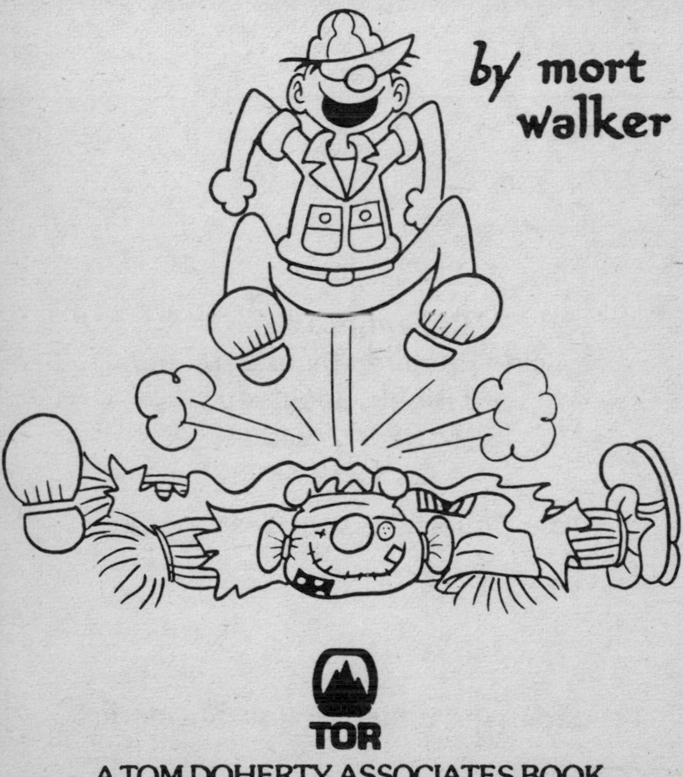

TOR
A TOM DOHERTY ASSOCIATES BOOK

ISBN: US 812-560868
CAN 812-560876

A Tom Doherty Associates Original

Printed in the United States of America

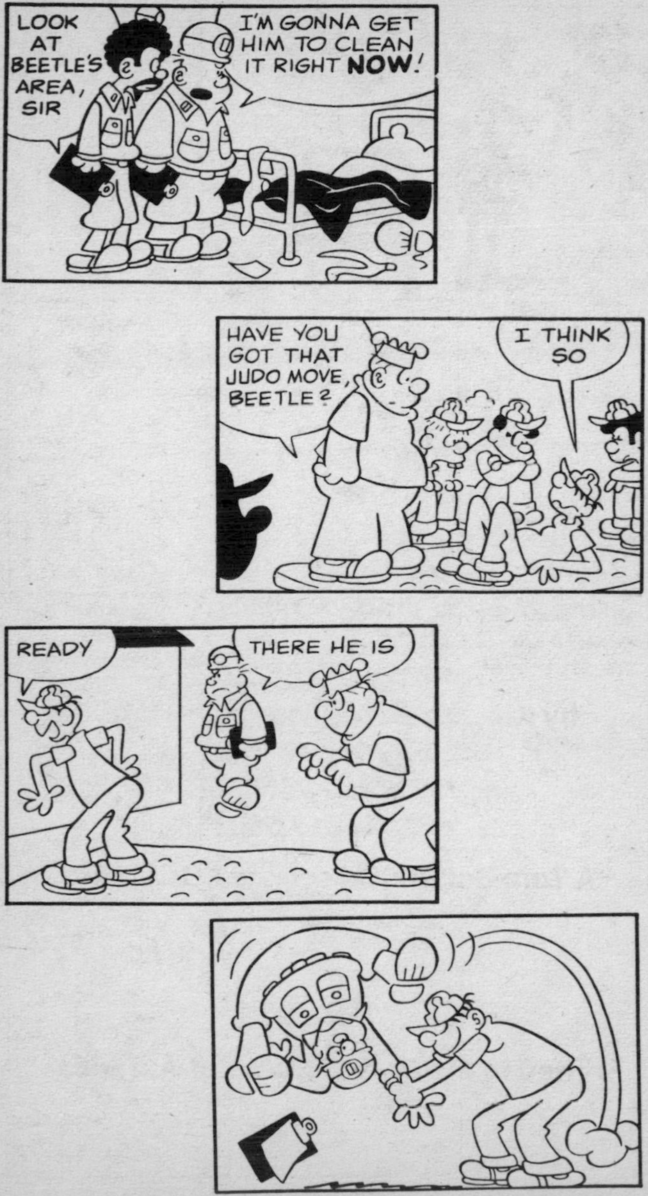
LOOK AT BEETLE'S AREA, SIR
I'M GONNA GET HIM TO CLEAN IT RIGHT **NOW**!
HAVE YOU GOT THAT JUDO MOVE, BEETLE?
I THINK SO
READY
THERE HE IS

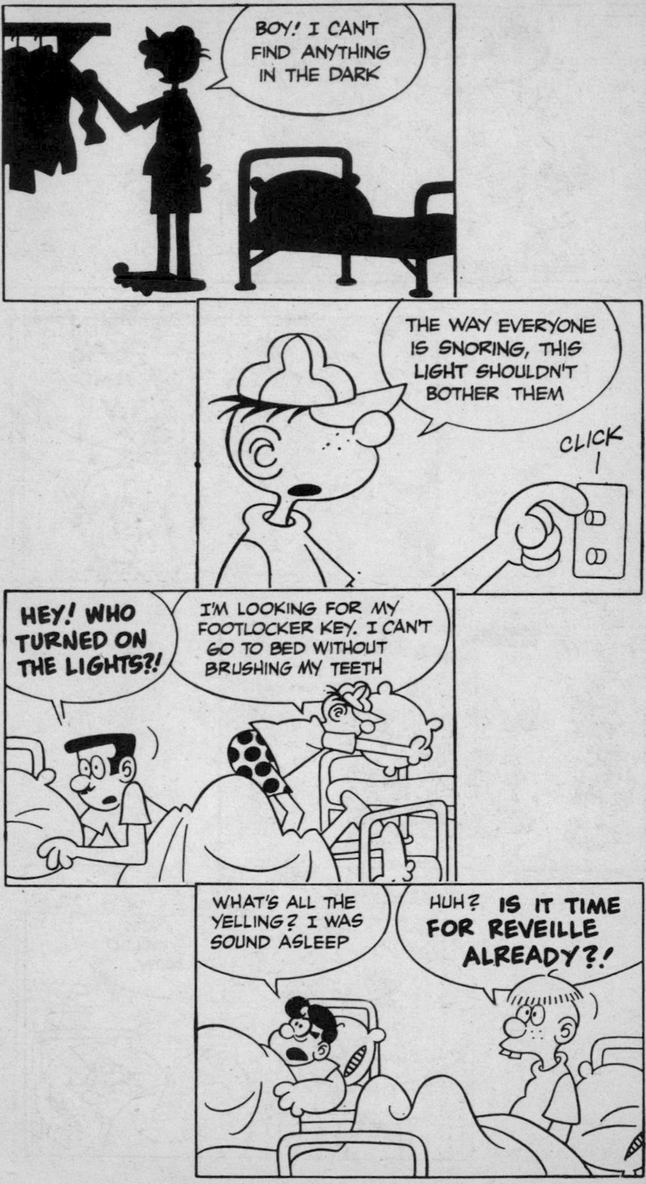
BOY! I CAN'T FIND ANYTHING IN THE DARK
THE WAY EVERYONE IS SNORING, THIS LIGHT SHOULDN'T BOTHER THEM
CLICK
HEY! WHO TURNED ON THE LIGHTS?!
I'M LOOKING FOR MY FOOTLOCKER KEY. I CAN'T GO TO BED WITHOUT BRUSHING MY TEETH
WHAT'S ALL THE YELLING? I WAS SOUND ASLEEP
HUH? IS IT TIME FOR REVEILLE ALREADY?!

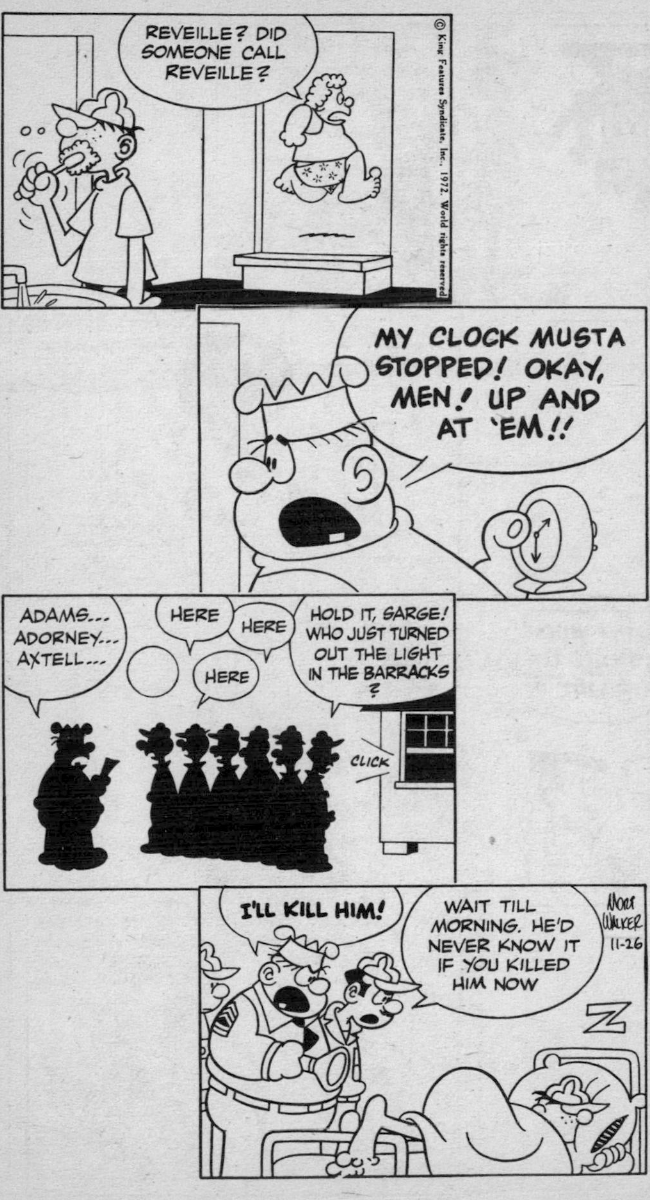
REVEILLE? DID SOMEONE CALL REVEILLE?
© King Features Syndicate, Inc., 1972. World rights reserved
MY CLOCK MUSTA STOPPED! OKAY, MEN! UP AND AT 'EM!!
ADAMS... ADORNEY... AXTELL...
HERE
HERE
HERE
HOLD IT, SARGE! WHO JUST TURNED OUT THE LIGHT IN THE BARRACKS?
CLICK
I'LL KILL HIM!
WAIT TILL MORNING. HE'D NEVER KNOW IT IF YOU KILLED HIM NOW
MORT WALKER 11-26
Z

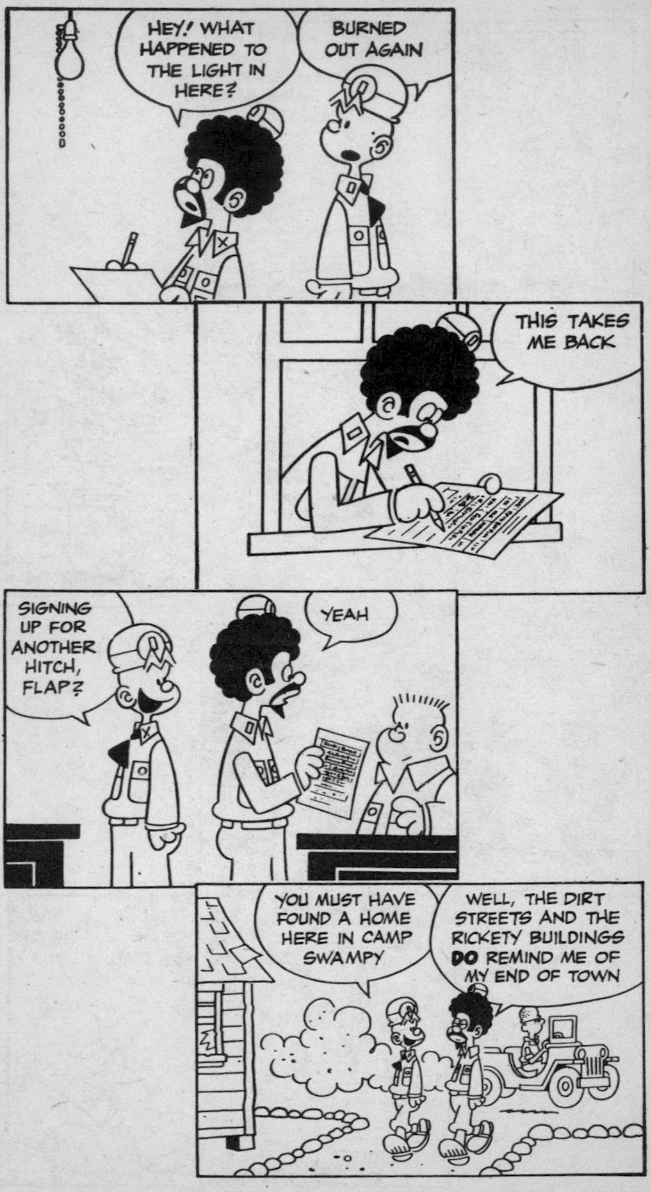
HEY! WHAT HAPPENED TO THE LIGHT IN HERE?
BURNED OUT AGAIN
THIS TAKES ME BACK
SIGNING UP FOR ANOTHER HITCH, FLAP?
YEAH
YOU MUST HAVE FOUND A HOME HERE IN CAMP SWAMPY
WELL, THE DIRT STREETS AND THE RICKETY BUILDINGS **DO** REMIND ME OF MY END OF TOWN

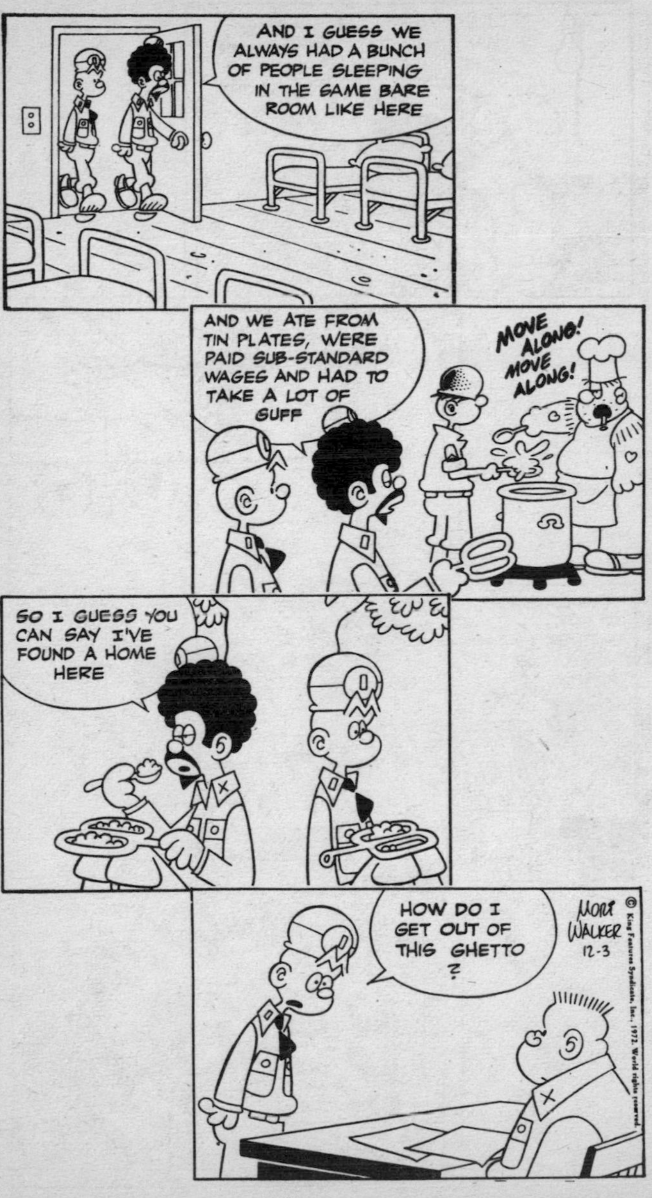
AND I GUESS WE ALWAYS HAD A BUNCH OF PEOPLE SLEEPING IN THE SAME BARE ROOM LIKE HERE
AND WE ATE FROM TIN PLATES, WERE PAID SUB-STANDARD WAGES AND HAD TO TAKE A LOT OF SUFF
MOVE ALONG! MOVE ALONG!
SO I GUESS YOU CAN SAY I'VE FOUND A HOME HERE
HOW DO I GET OUT OF THIS GHETTO ?
MORT WALKER 12-3
© King Features Syndicate, Inc., 1972. World rights reserved.

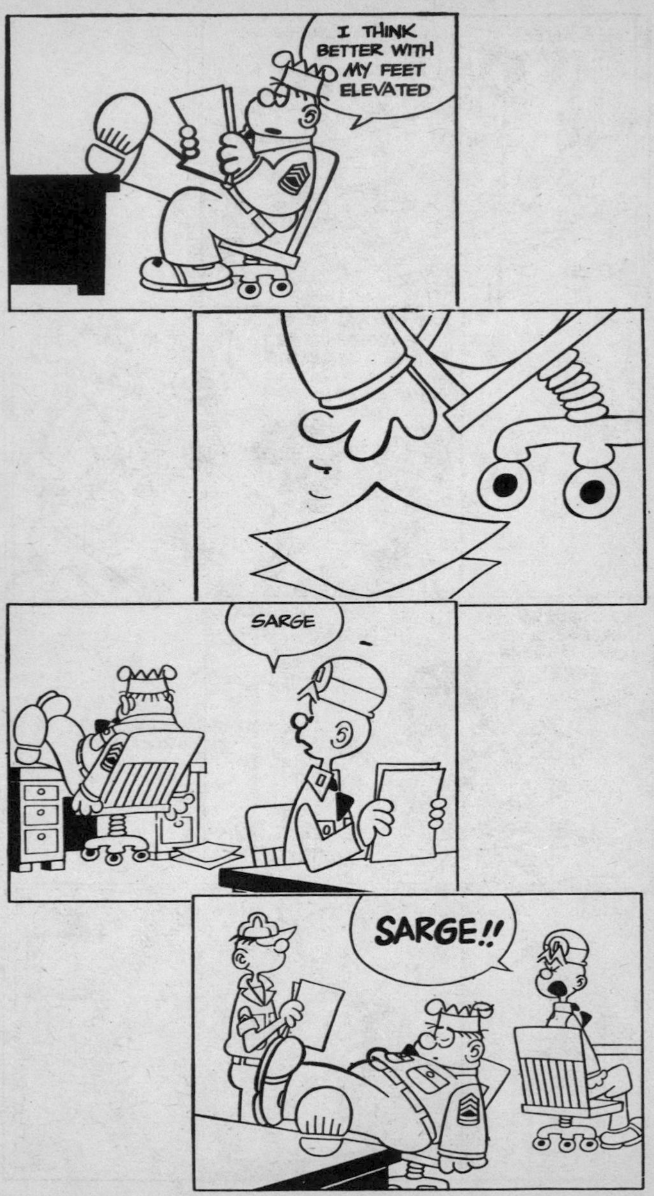
I THINK BETTER WITH MY FEET ELEVATED
SARGE
SARGE!!

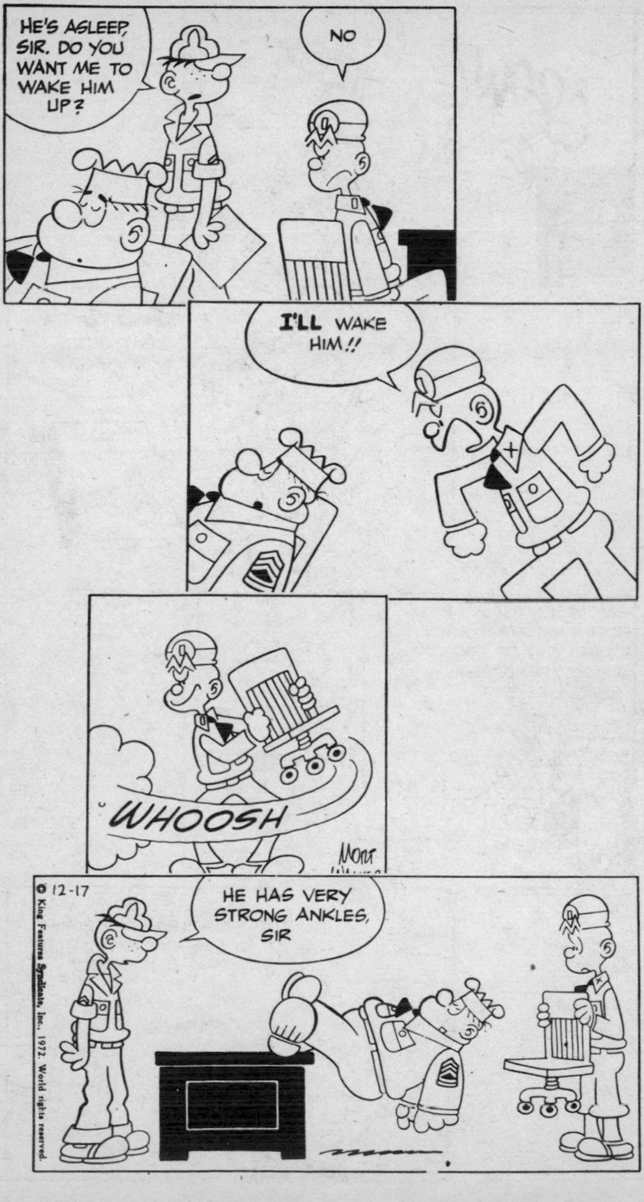
HE'S ASLEEP, SIR. DO YOU WANT ME TO WAKE HIM UP?
NO
I'LL WAKE HIM!!
WHOOSH
MORT WALKER
© 12-17
King Features Syndicate, Inc., 1972. World rights reserved.
HE HAS VERY STRONG ANKLES, SIR

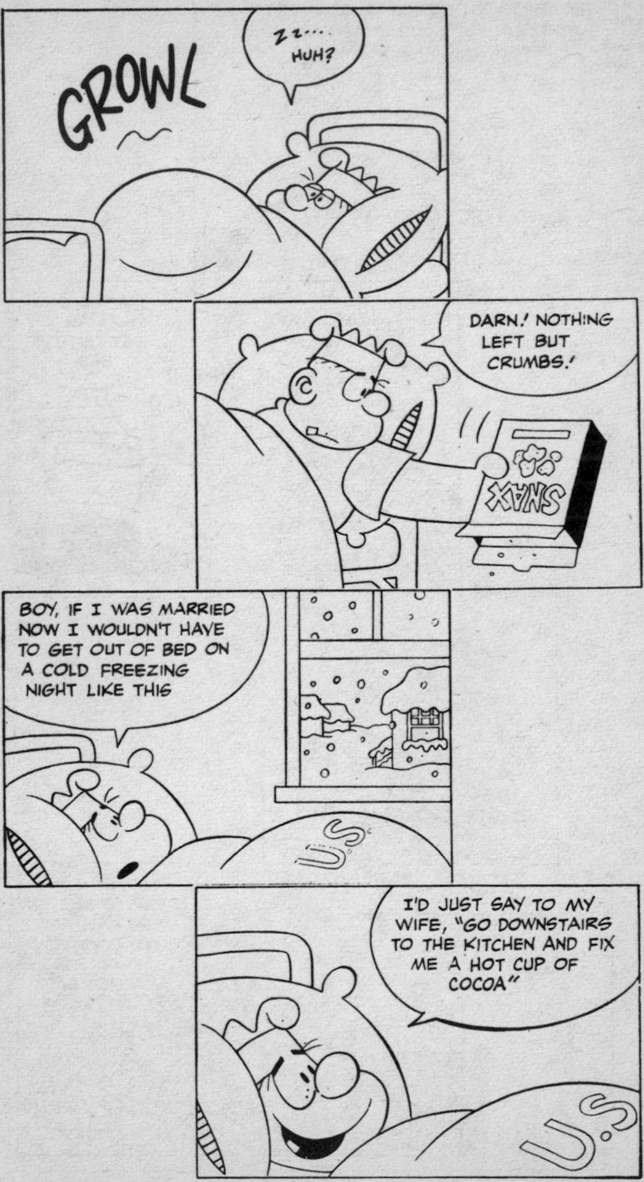
GROWL
ZZ... HUH?
DARN! NOTHING LEFT BUT CRUMBS!
SNAX
BOY, IF I WAS MARRIED NOW I WOULDN'T HAVE TO GET OUT OF BED ON A COLD FREEZING NIGHT LIKE THIS
U.S
I'D JUST SAY TO MY WIFE, "GO DOWNSTAIRS TO THE KITCHEN AND FIX ME A HOT CUP OF COCOA"
U.S

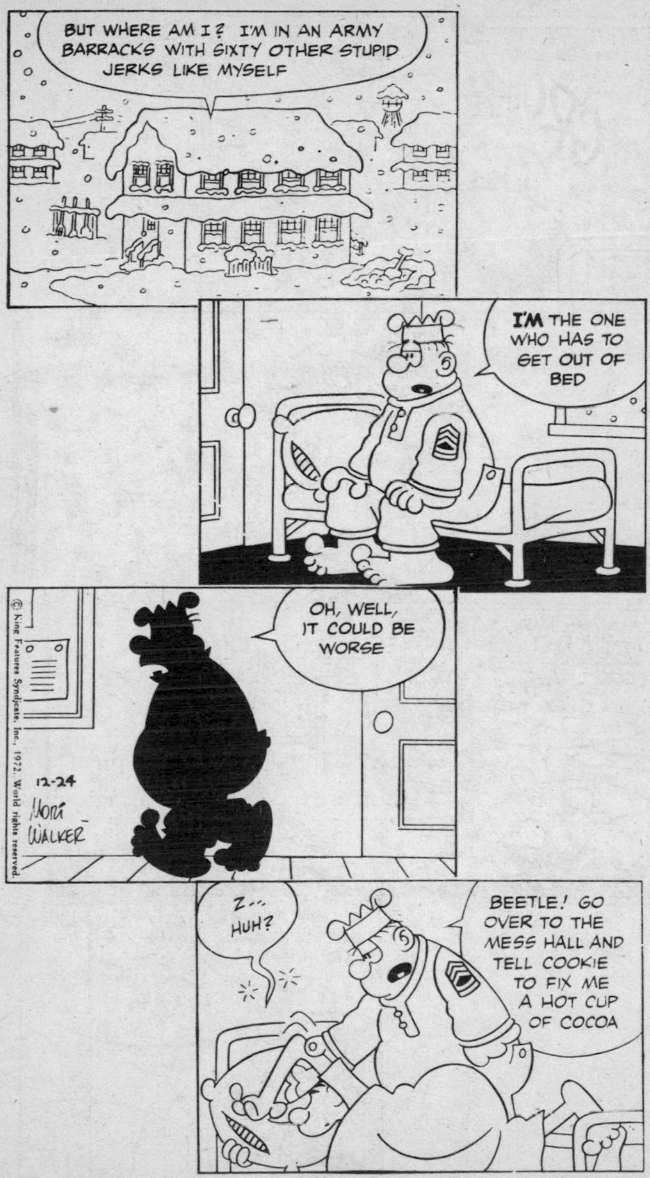
BUT WHERE AM I? I'M IN AN ARMY BARRACKS WITH SIXTY OTHER STUPID JERKS LIKE MYSELF
I'M THE ONE WHO HAS TO GET OUT OF BED
OH, WELL, IT COULD BE WORSE
© King Features Syndicate, Inc., 1972. World rights reserved.
12-24
MORT WALKER
Z-.. HUH?
BEETLE! GO OVER TO THE MESS HALL AND TELL COOKIE TO FIX ME A HOT CUP OF COCOA

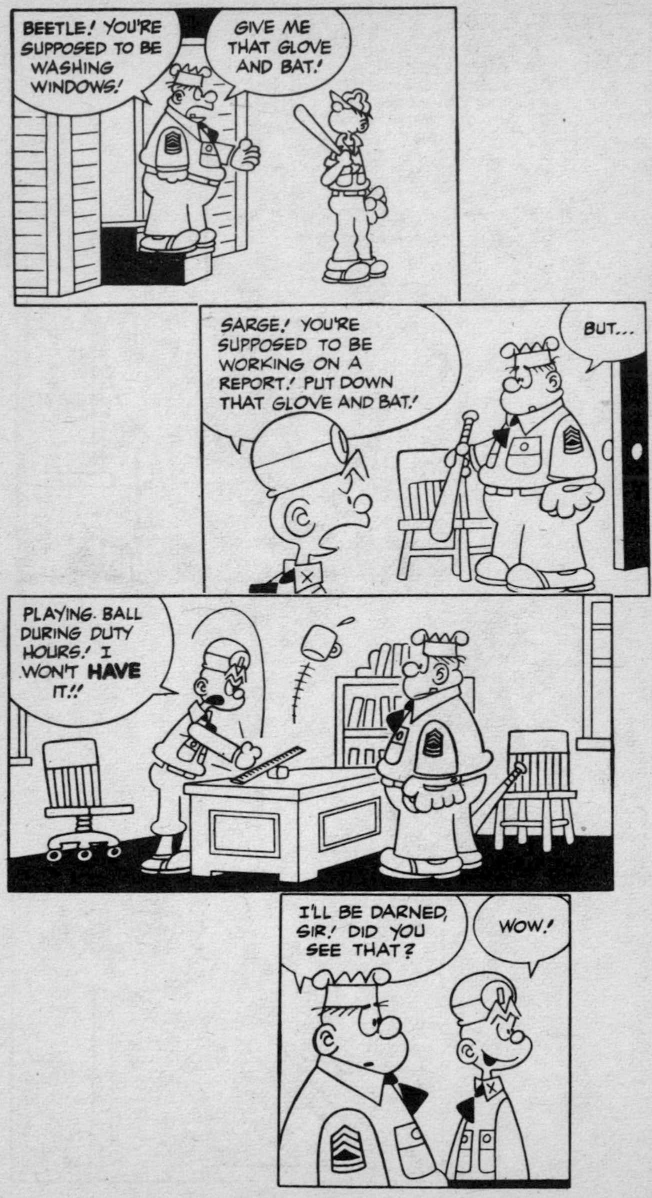
BEETLE! YOU'RE SUPPOSED TO BE WASHING WINDOWS!
GIVE ME THAT GLOVE AND BAT!
SARGE! YOU'RE SUPPOSED TO BE WORKING ON A REPORT! PUT DOWN THAT GLOVE AND BAT!
BUT...
PLAYING BALL DURING DUTY HOURS! I WON'T HAVE IT!!
I'LL BE DARNED, SIR! DID YOU SEE THAT?
WOW!

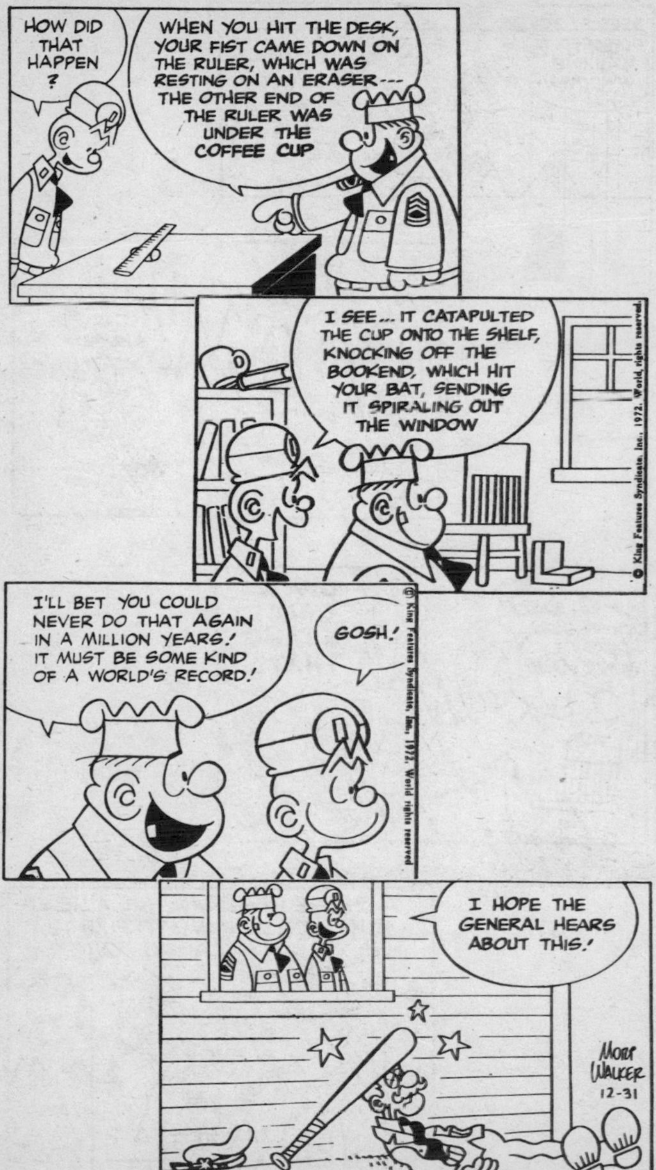
HOW DID THAT HAPPEN ?
WHEN YOU HIT THE DESK, YOUR FIST CAME DOWN ON THE RULER, WHICH WAS RESTING ON AN ERASER--- THE OTHER END OF THE RULER WAS UNDER THE COFFEE CUP
I SEE... IT CATAPULTED THE CUP ONTO THE SHELF, KNOCKING OFF THE BOOKEND, WHICH HIT YOUR BAT, SENDING IT SPIRALING OUT THE WINDOW
© King Features Syndicate, Inc., 1972. World rights reserved.
I'LL BET YOU COULD NEVER DO THAT AGAIN IN A MILLION YEARS! IT MUST BE SOME KIND OF A WORLD'S RECORD!
GOSH!
I HOPE THE GENERAL HEARS ABOUT THIS!
MORT WALKER
12-31

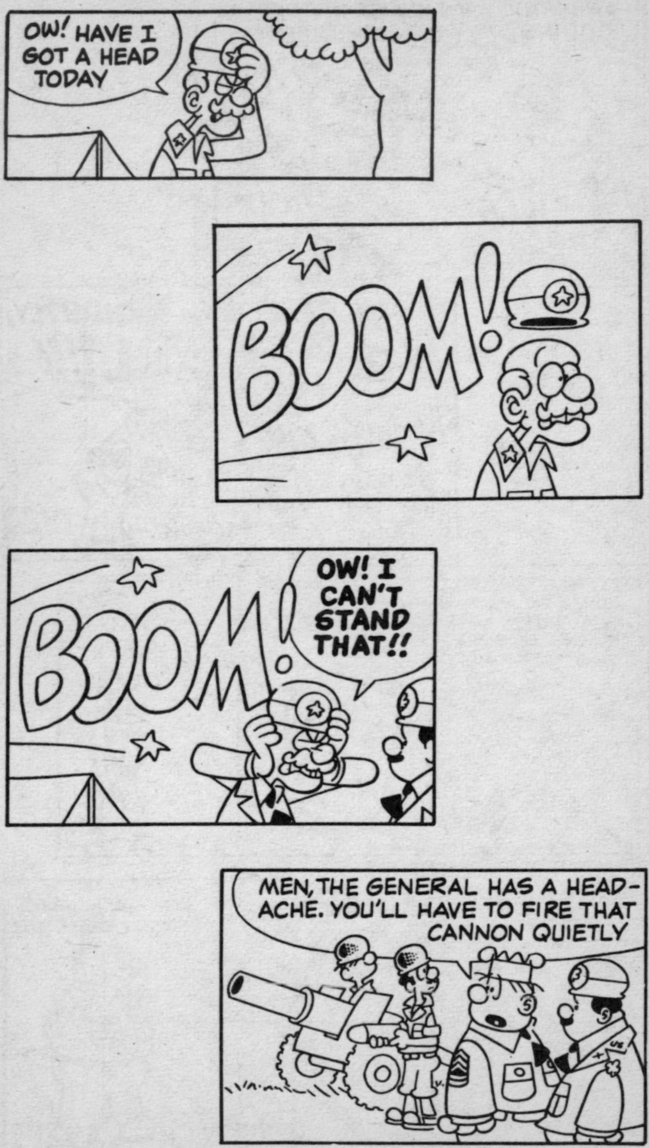
OW! HAVE I GOT A HEAD TODAY
BOOM!
BOOM!
OW! I CAN'T STAND THAT!!
MEN, THE GENERAL HAS A HEAD-ACHE. YOU'LL HAVE TO FIRE THAT CANNON QUIETLY

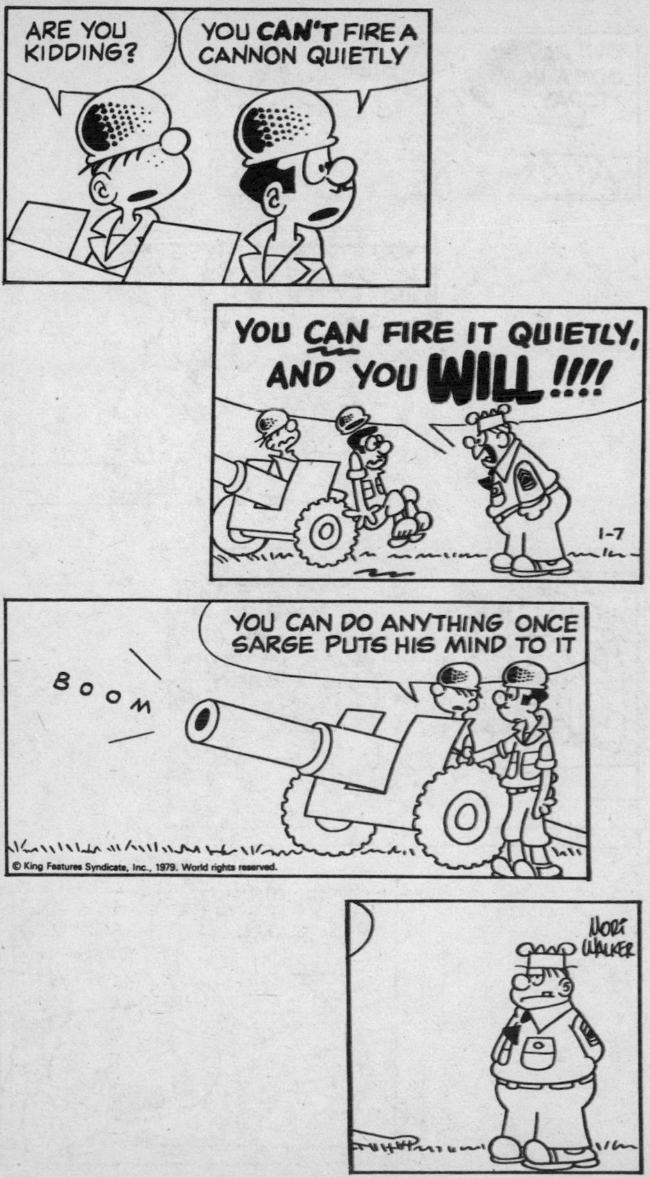
ARE YOU KIDDING?
YOU CAN'T FIRE A CANNON QUIETLY
YOU CAN FIRE IT QUIETLY, AND YOU WILL!!!!
1-7
YOU CAN DO ANYTHING ONCE SARGE PUTS HIS MIND TO IT
BOOM
MORT WALKER

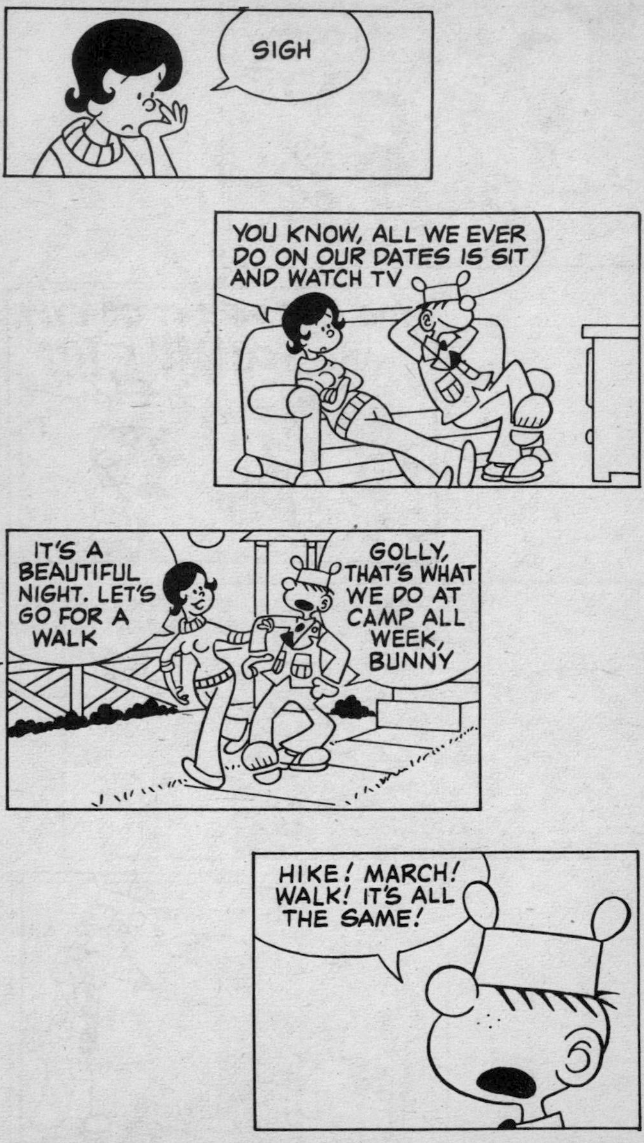

SIGH
YOU KNOW, ALL WE EVER DO ON OUR DATES IS SIT AND WATCH TV
IT'S A BEAUTIFUL NIGHT. LET'S GO FOR A WALK
GOLLY, THAT'S WHAT WE DO AT CAMP ALL WEEK, BUNNY
HIKE! MARCH! WALK! IT'S ALL THE SAME!

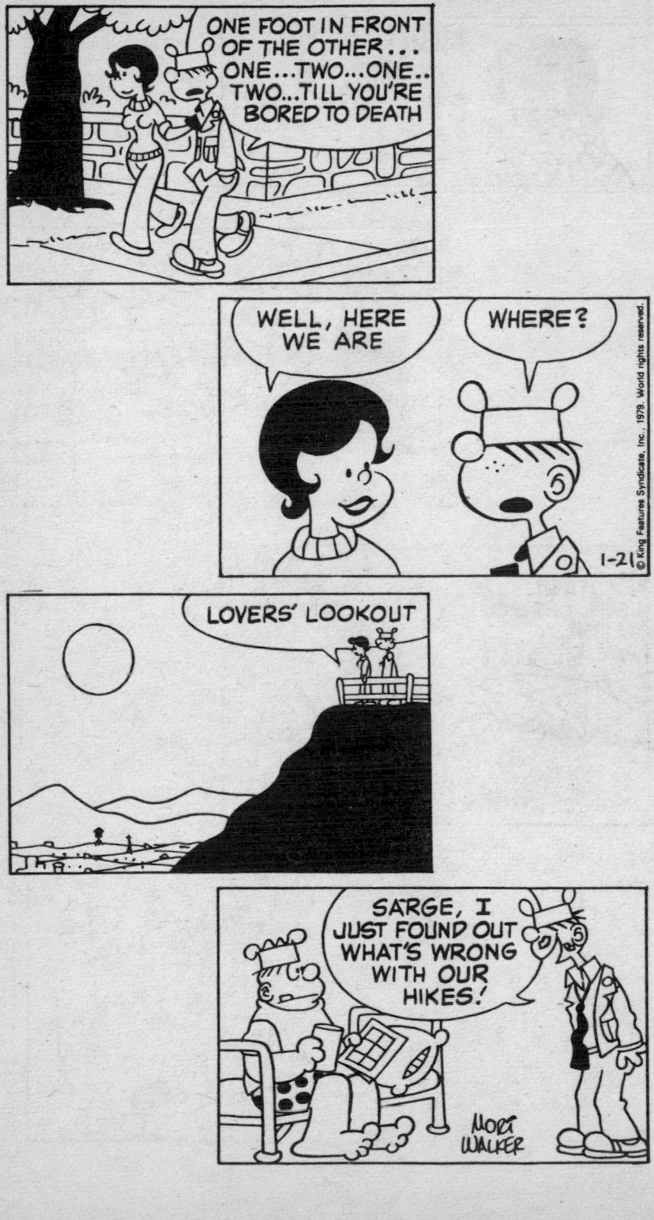
ONE FOOT IN FRONT OF THE OTHER... ONE...TWO...ONE.. TWO...TILL YOU'RE BORED TO DEATH
WELL, HERE WE ARE
WHERE?
1-21
© King Features Syndicate, Inc., 1979. World rights reserved.
LOVERS' LOOKOUT
SARGE, I JUST FOUND OUT WHAT'S WRONG WITH OUR HIKES!
MORT WALKER

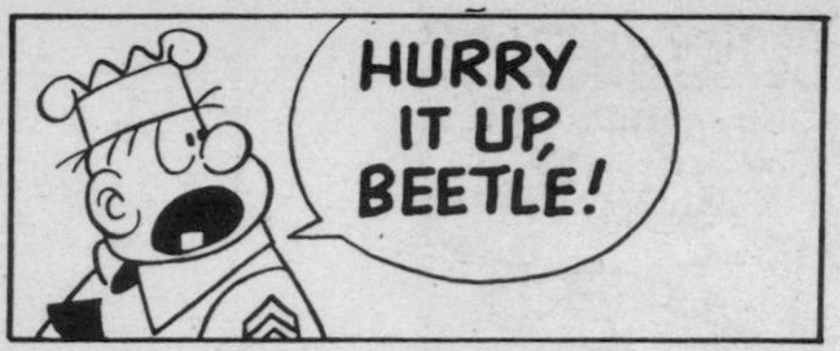
HURRY IT UP, BEETLE!

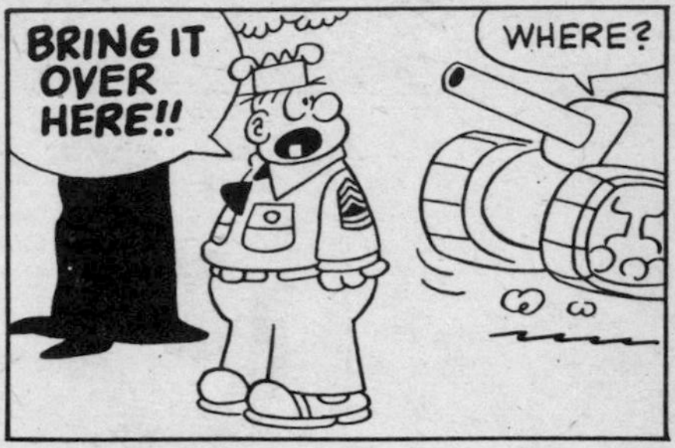
BRING IT OVER HERE!!
WHERE?

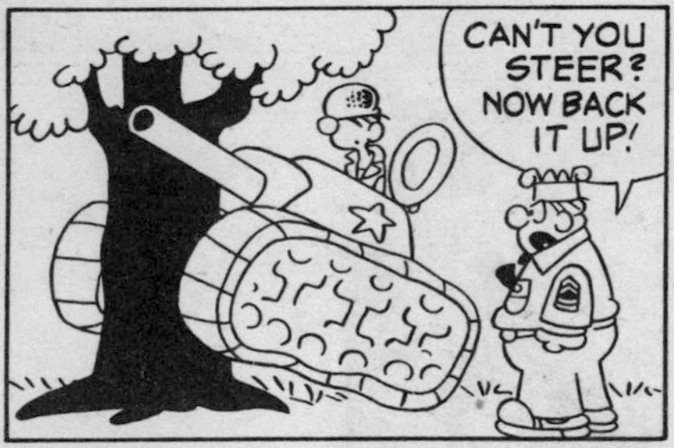
CAN'T YOU STEER? NOW BACK IT UP!

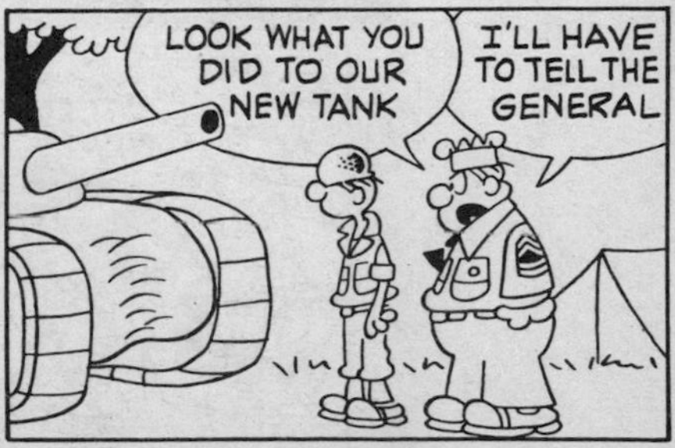
LOOK WHAT YOU DID TO OUR NEW TANK
I'LL HAVE TO TELL THE GENERAL

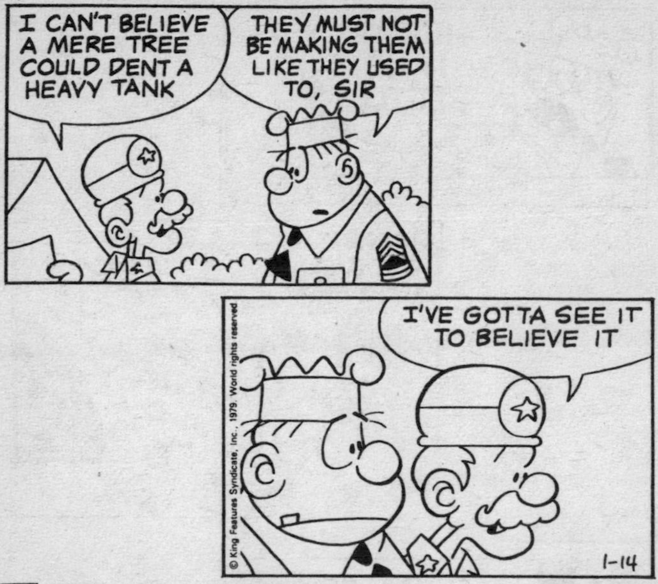
I CAN'T BELIEVE A MERE TREE COULD DENT A HEAVY TANK
THEY MUST NOT BE MAKING THEM LIKE THEY USED TO, SIR
© King Features Syndicate, Inc., 1979. World rights reserved
I'VE GOTTA SEE IT TO BELIEVE IT
1-14

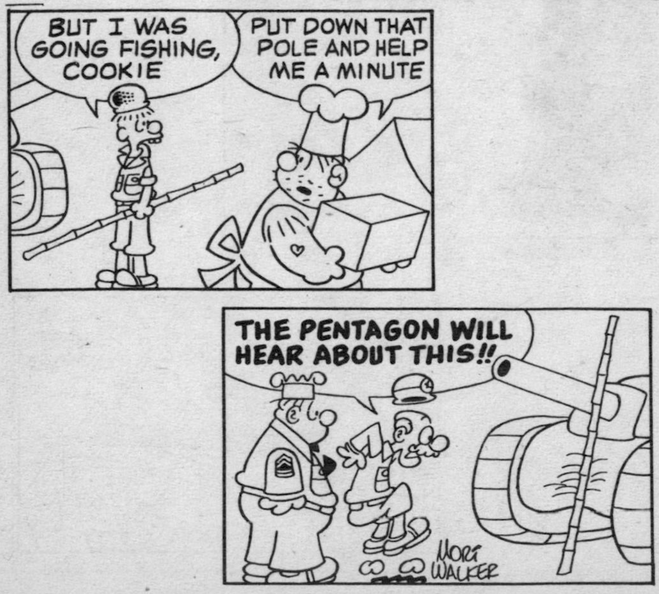
BUT I WAS GOING FISHING, COOKIE
PUT DOWN THAT POLE AND HELP ME A MINUTE
THE PENTAGON WILL HEAR ABOUT THIS!!
MORT WALKER

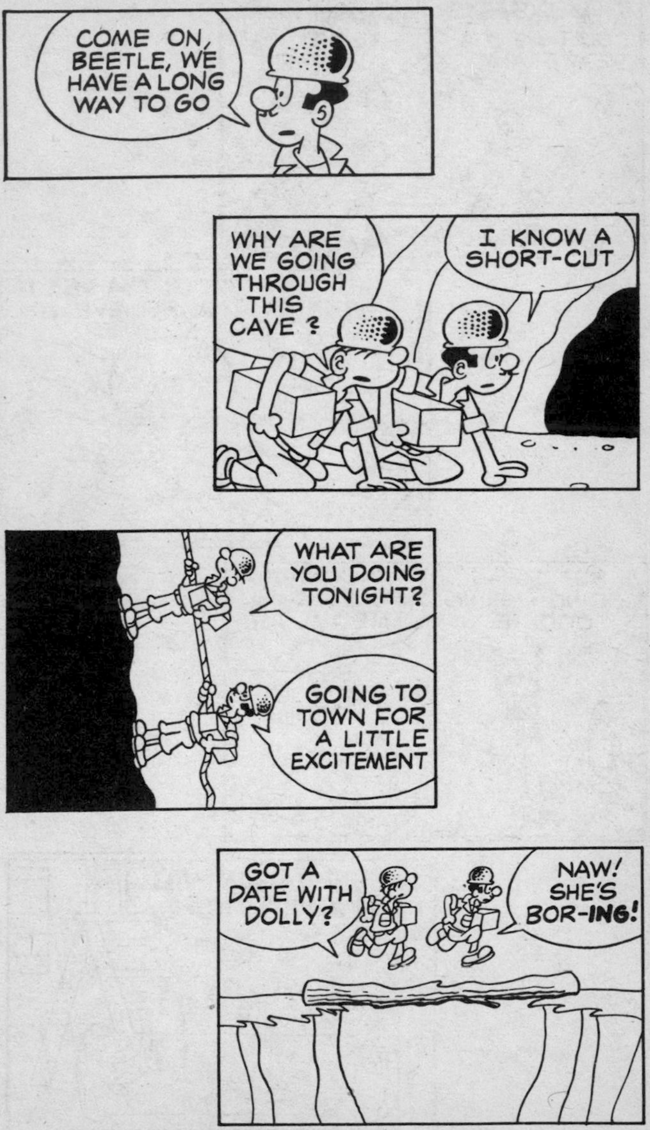
COME ON, BEETLE, WE HAVE A LONG WAY TO GO
WHY ARE WE GOING THROUGH THIS CAVE ?
I KNOW A SHORT-CUT
WHAT ARE YOU DOING TONIGHT?
GOING TO TOWN FOR A LITTLE EXCITEMENT
GOT A DATE WITH DOLLY?
NAW! SHE'S BOR-**ING**!

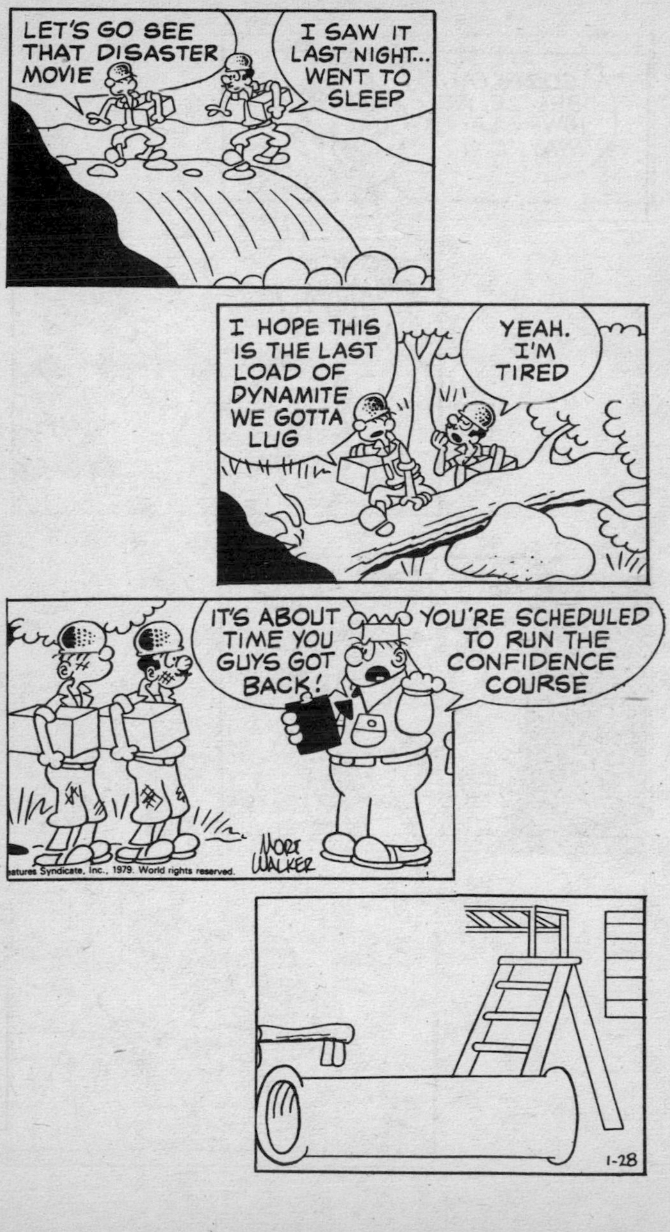
LET'S GO SEE THAT DISASTER MOVIE
I SAW IT LAST NIGHT... WENT TO SLEEP
I HOPE THIS IS THE LAST LOAD OF DYNAMITE WE GOTTA LUG
YEAH. I'M TIRED
IT'S ABOUT TIME YOU GUYS GOT BACK!
YOU'RE SCHEDULED TO RUN THE CONFIDENCE COURSE
MORT WALKER
atures Syndicate, Inc., 1979. World rights reserved.
1-28

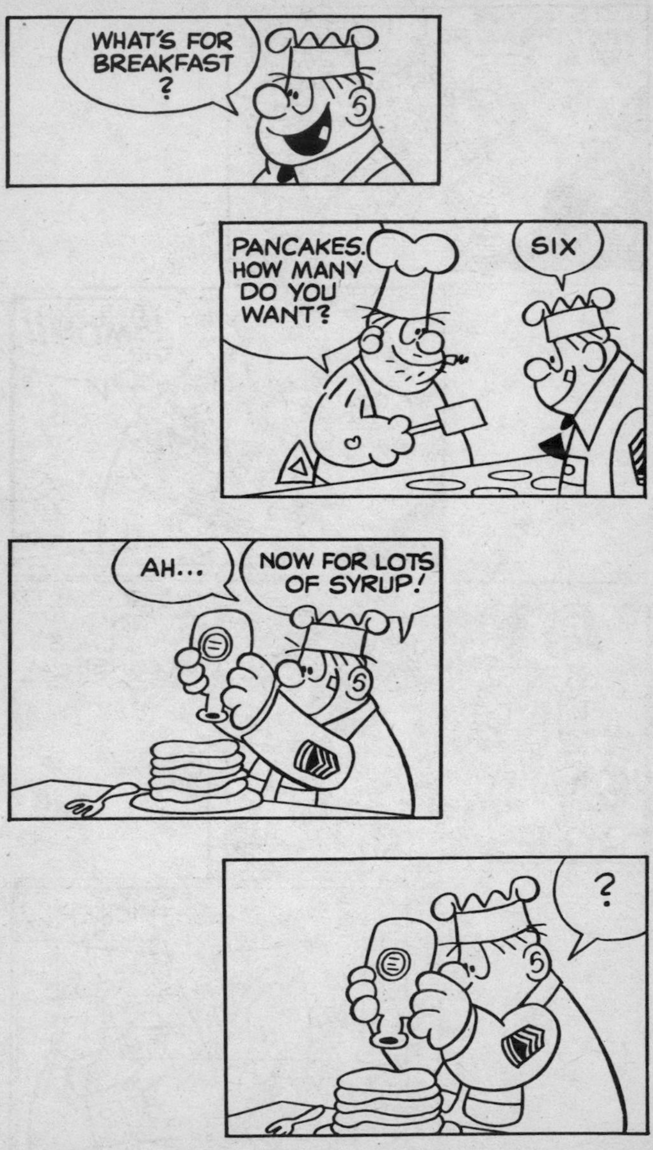
WHAT'S FOR BREAKFAST ?
PANCAKES. HOW MANY DO YOU WANT?
SIX
AH...
NOW FOR LOTS OF SYRUP!
?

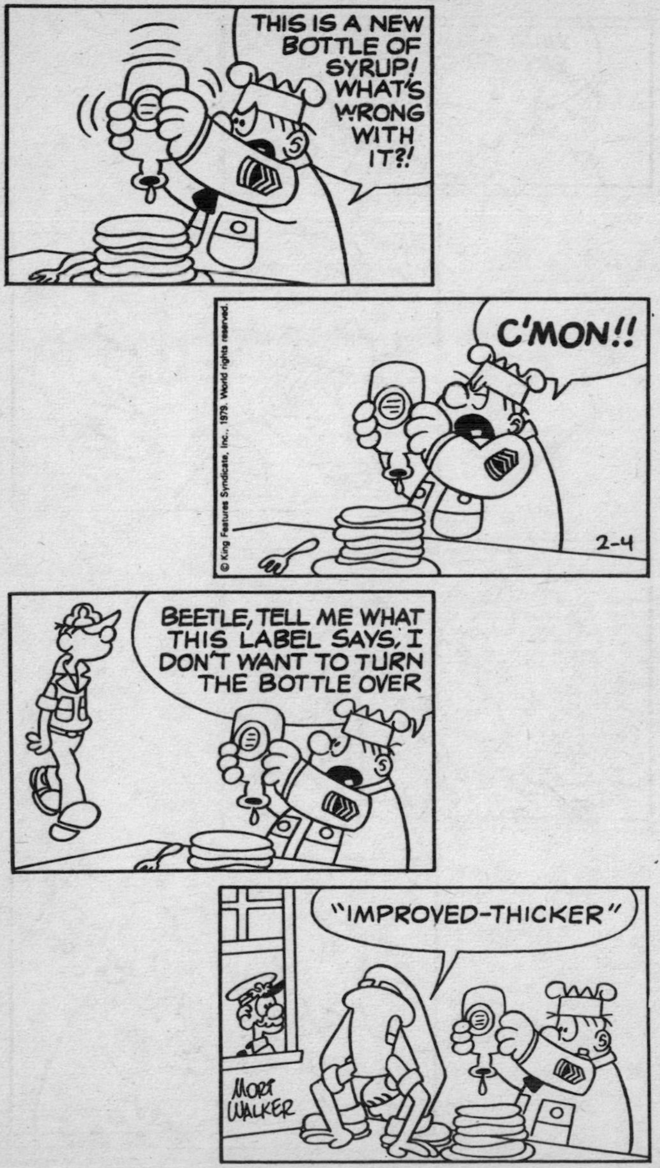
THIS IS A NEW BOTTLE OF SYRUP! WHAT'S WRONG WITH IT?!
C'MON!!
© King Features Syndicate, Inc., 1979. World rights reserved.
2-4
BEETLE, TELL ME WHAT THIS LABEL SAYS, I DON'T WANT TO TURN THE BOTTLE OVER
"IMPROVED-THICKER"
MORT WALKER

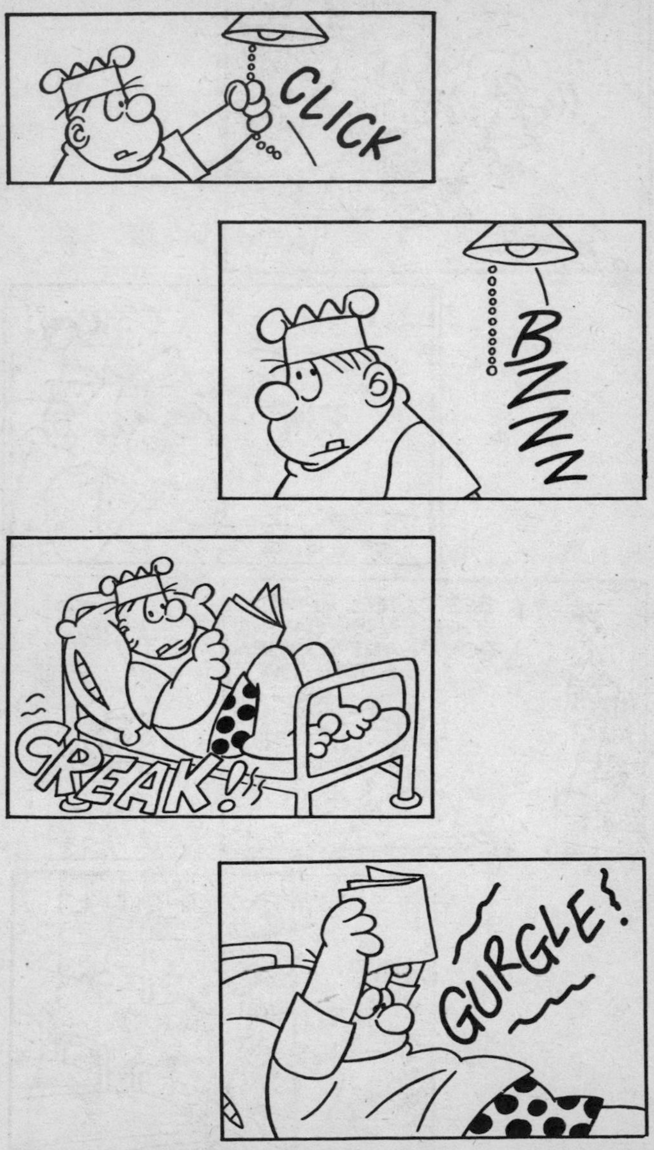
CLICK
BZZNN
CREAK!
GURGLE!

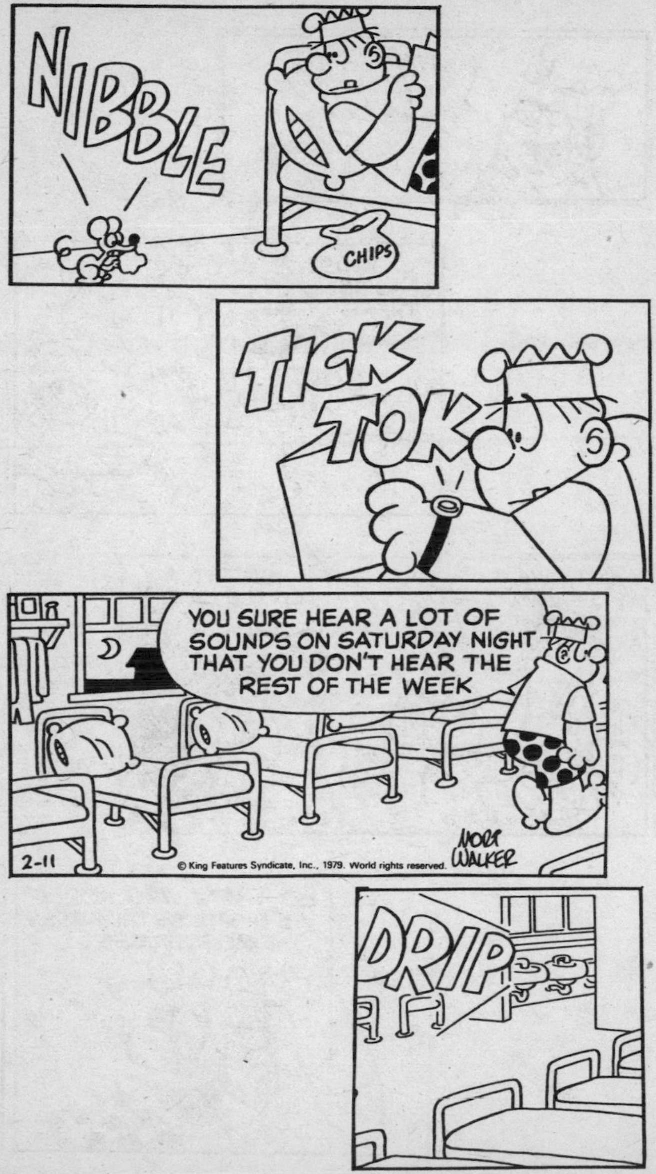
NIBBLE
CHIPS
TICK TOK
YOU SURE HEAR A LOT OF SOUNDS ON SATURDAY NIGHT THAT YOU DON'T HEAR THE REST OF THE WEEK
2-11
© King Features Syndicate, Inc., 1979. World rights reserved.
MORT WALKER
DRIP

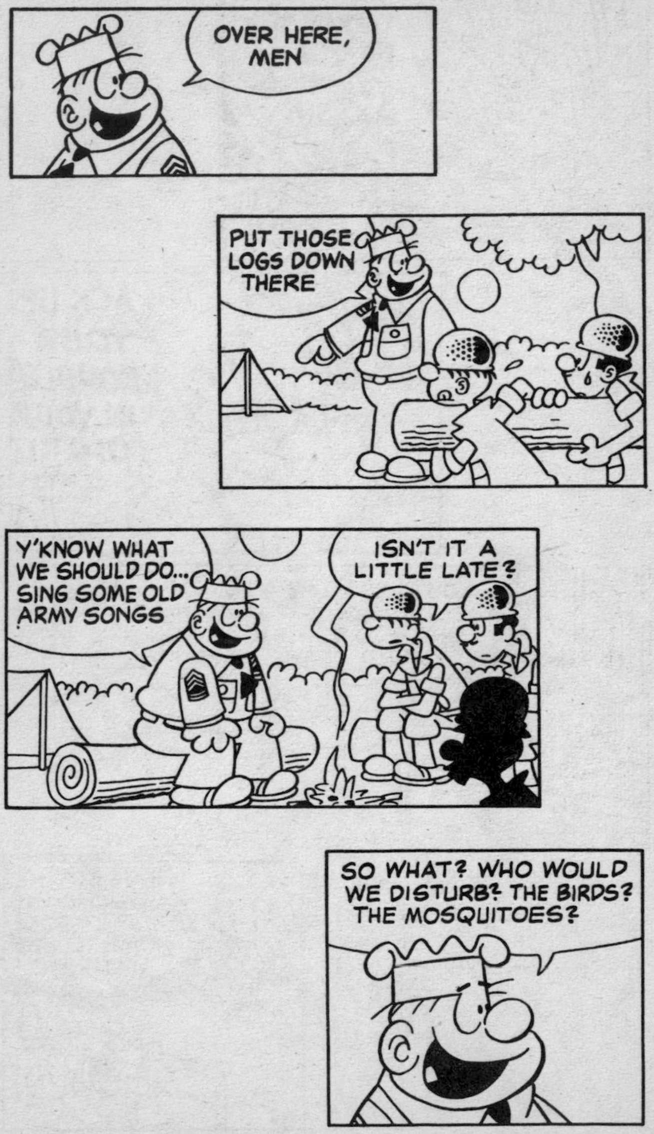
OVER HERE, MEN
PUT THOSE LOGS DOWN THERE
Y'KNOW WHAT WE SHOULD DO... SING SOME OLD ARMY SONGS
ISN'T IT A LITTLE LATE?
SO WHAT? WHO WOULD WE DISTURB? THE BIRDS? THE MOSQUITOES?

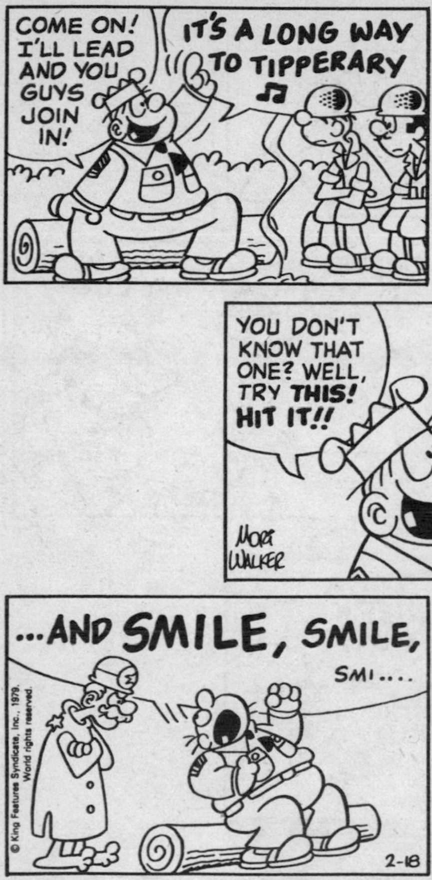
COME ON! I'LL LEAD AND YOU GUYS JOIN IN!
IT'S A LONG WAY TO TIPPERARY
YOU DON'T KNOW THAT ONE? WELL, TRY THIS! HIT IT!!
PACK UP YOUR TROUBLES IN YOUR OLD KIT BAG
MORT WALKER
...AND SMILE, SMILE,
SMI....
© King Features Syndicate, Inc., 1979. World rights reserved.
2-18

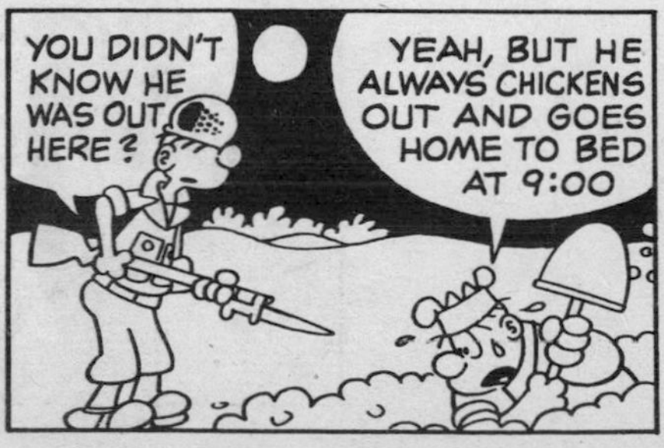
YOU DIDN'T KNOW HE WAS OUT HERE?
YEAH, BUT HE ALWAYS CHICKENS OUT AND GOES HOME TO BED AT 9:00

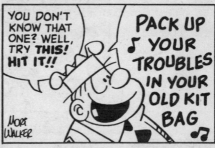

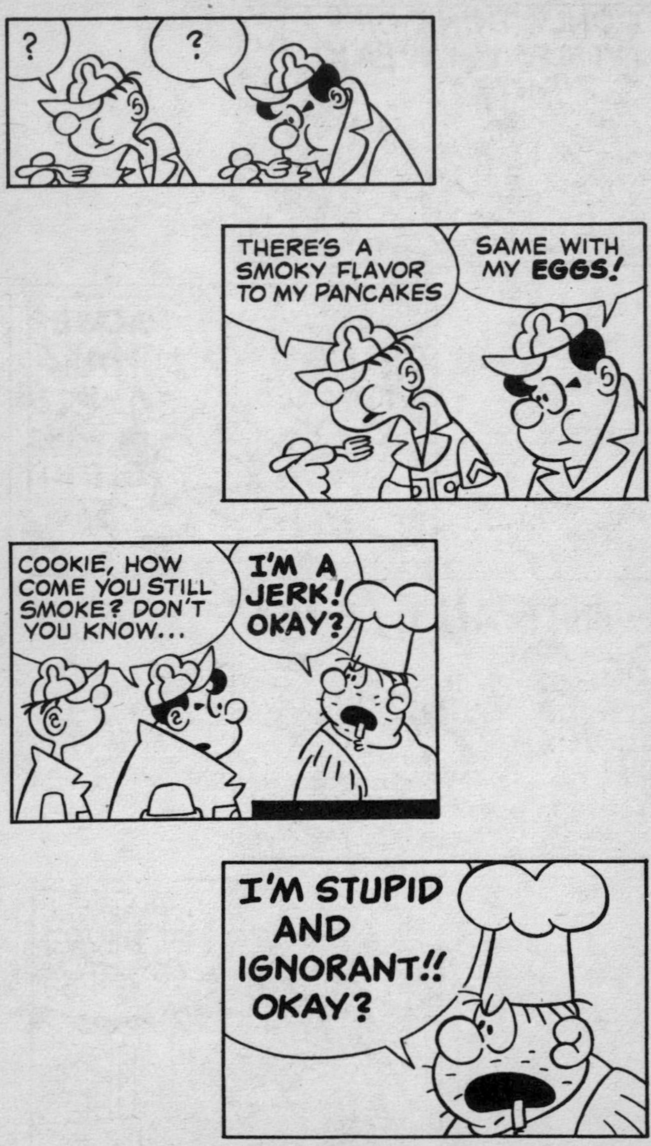
?
?
THERE'S A SMOKY FLAVOR TO MY PANCAKES
SAME WITH MY **EGGS!**
COOKIE, HOW COME YOU STILL SMOKE? DON'T YOU KNOW...
I'M A JERK! OKAY?
I'M STUPID AND IGNORANT!! OKAY?

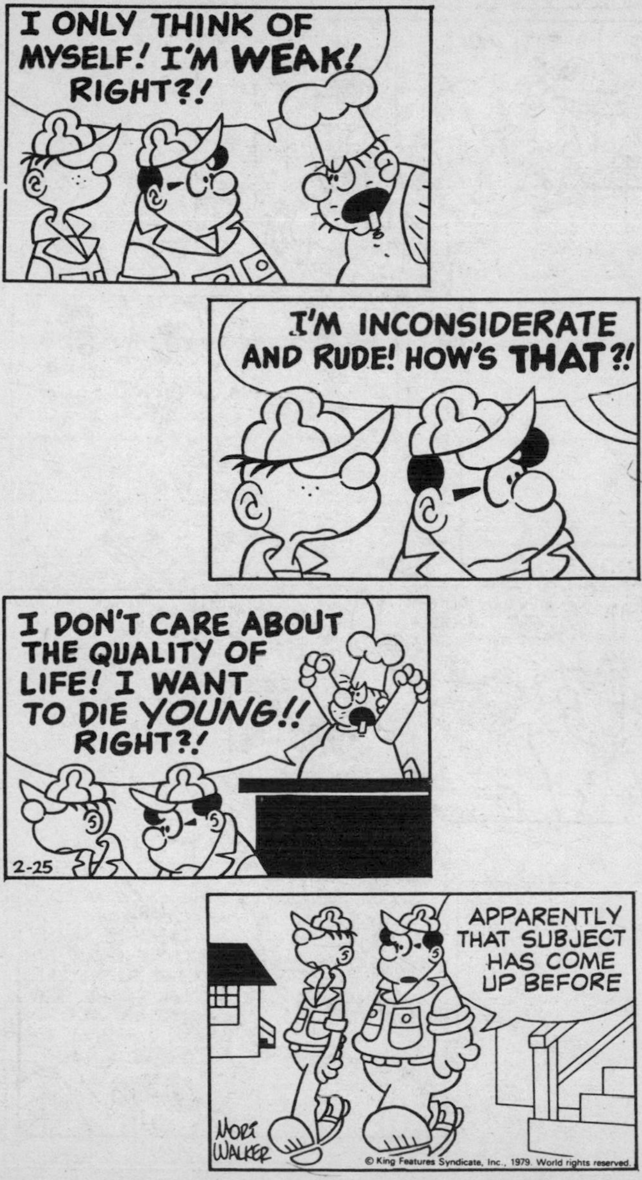
I ONLY THINK OF MYSELF! I'M WEAK! RIGHT?!
I'M INCONSIDERATE AND RUDE! HOW'S THAT?!
I DON'T CARE ABOUT THE QUALITY OF LIFE! I WANT TO DIE YOUNG!! RIGHT?!
2-25
APPARENTLY THAT SUBJECT HAS COME UP BEFORE
MORT WALKER
© King Features Syndicate, Inc., 1979. World rights reserved.

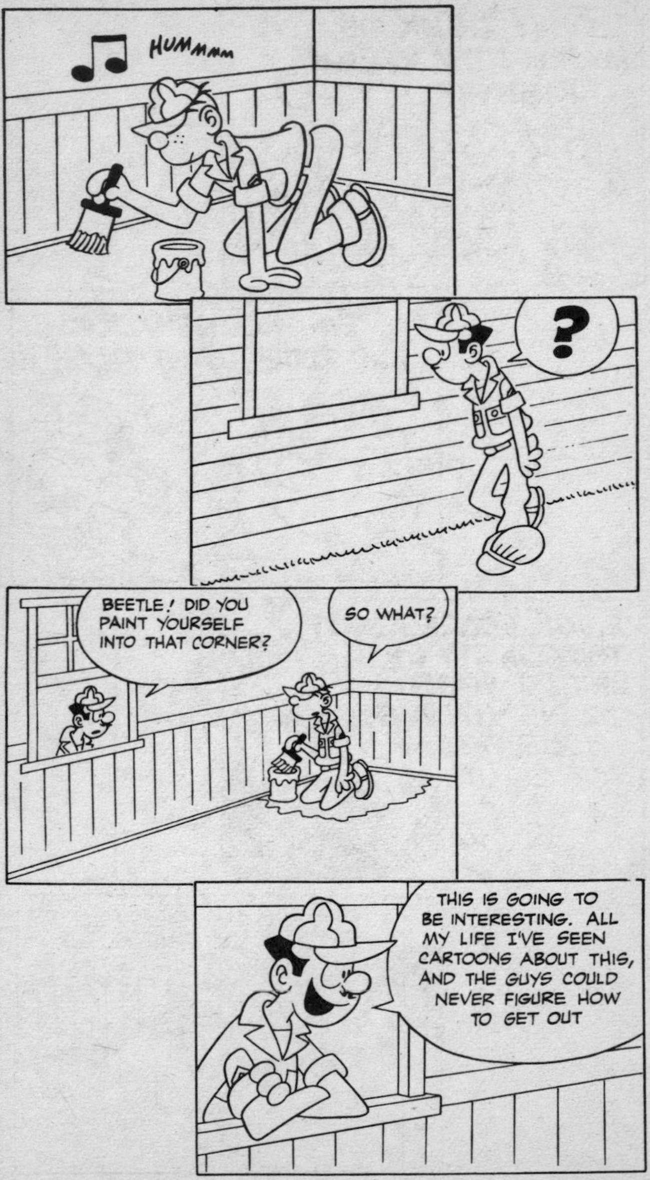
HUMmmm
?
BEETLE! DID YOU PAINT YOURSELF INTO THAT CORNER?
SO WHAT?
THIS IS GOING TO BE INTERESTING. ALL MY LIFE I'VE SEEN CARTOONS ABOUT THIS, AND THE GUYS COULD NEVER FIGURE HOW TO GET OUT

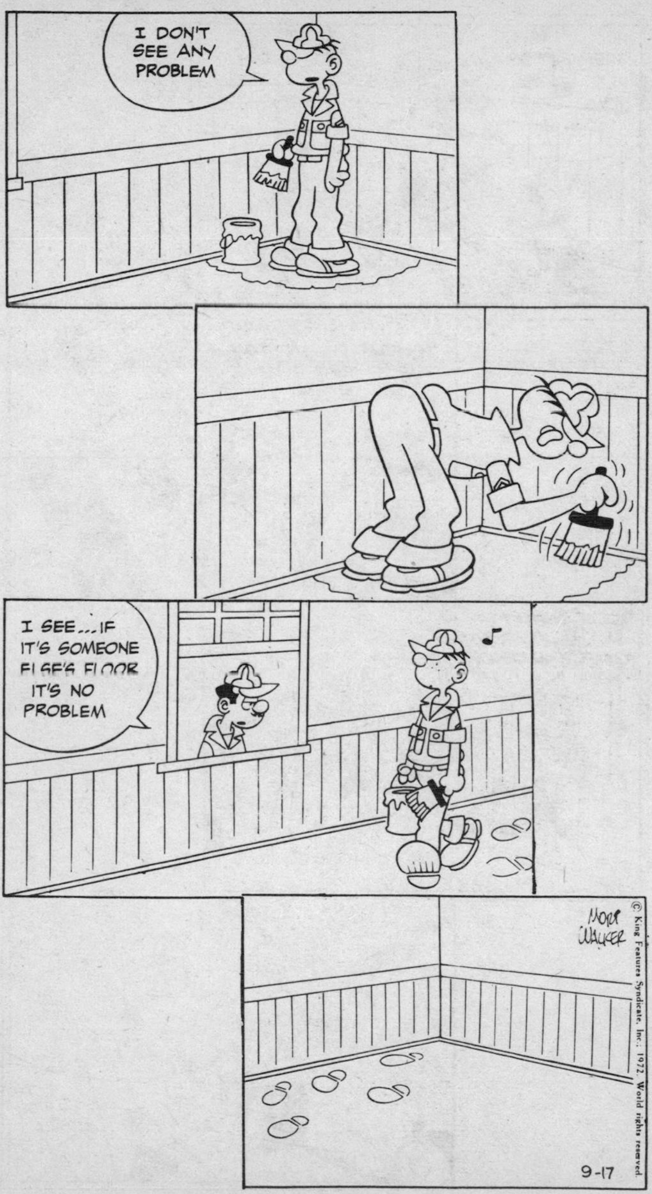

I DON'T SEE ANY PROBLEM
I SEE...IF IT'S SOMEONE ELSE'S FLOOR IT'S NO PROBLEM
MORT WALKER
© King Features Syndicate, Inc., 1972. World rights reserved.
9-17

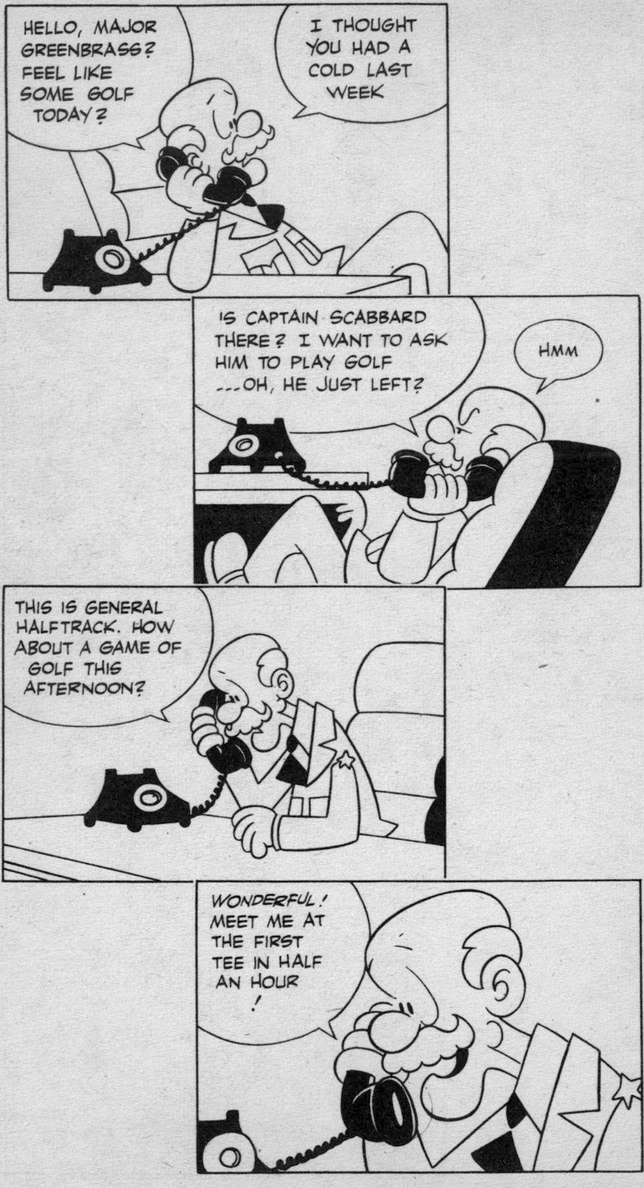
HELLO, MAJOR GREENBRASS? FEEL LIKE SOME GOLF TODAY?
I THOUGHT YOU HAD A COLD LAST WEEK
IS CAPTAIN SCABBARD THERE? I WANT TO ASK HIM TO PLAY GOLF ---OH, HE JUST LEFT?
HMM
THIS IS GENERAL HALFTRACK. HOW ABOUT A GAME OF GOLF THIS AFTERNOON?
WONDERFUL! MEET ME AT THE FIRST TEE IN HALF AN HOUR!

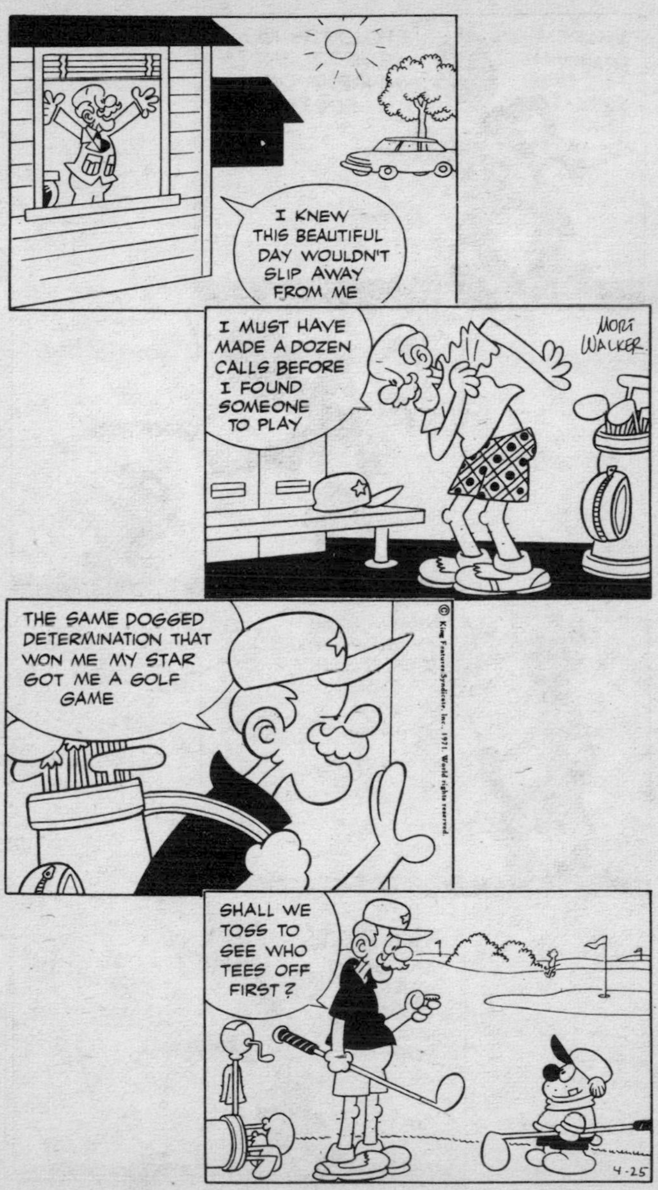
I KNEW THIS BEAUTIFUL DAY WOULDN'T SLIP AWAY FROM ME
I MUST HAVE MADE A DOZEN CALLS BEFORE I FOUND SOMEONE TO PLAY
MORT WALKER
THE SAME DOGGED DETERMINATION THAT WON ME MY STAR GOT ME A GOLF GAME
© King Features Syndicate, Inc., 1971. World rights reserved.
SHALL WE TOSS TO SEE WHO TEES OFF FIRST?
4-25

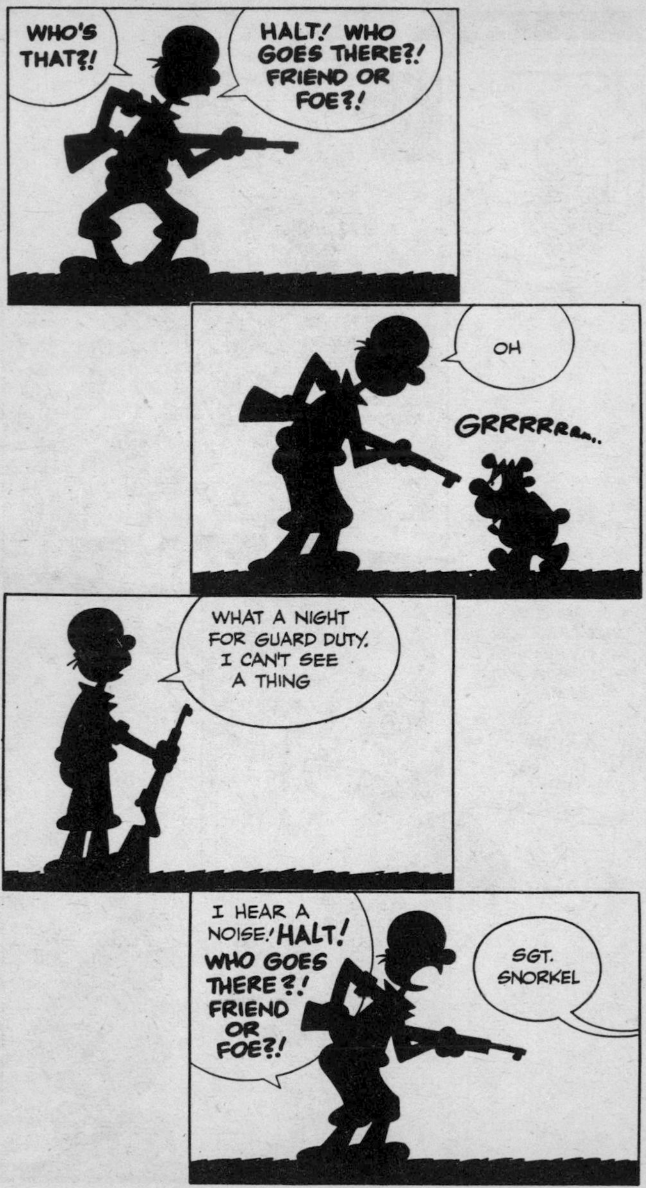
WHO'S THAT?!
HALT! WHO GOES THERE?! FRIEND OR FOE?!
OH
GRRRRR..
WHAT A NIGHT FOR GUARD DUTY. I CAN'T SEE A THING
I HEAR A NOISE! HALT! WHO GOES THERE?! FRIEND OR FOE?!
SGT. SNORKEL

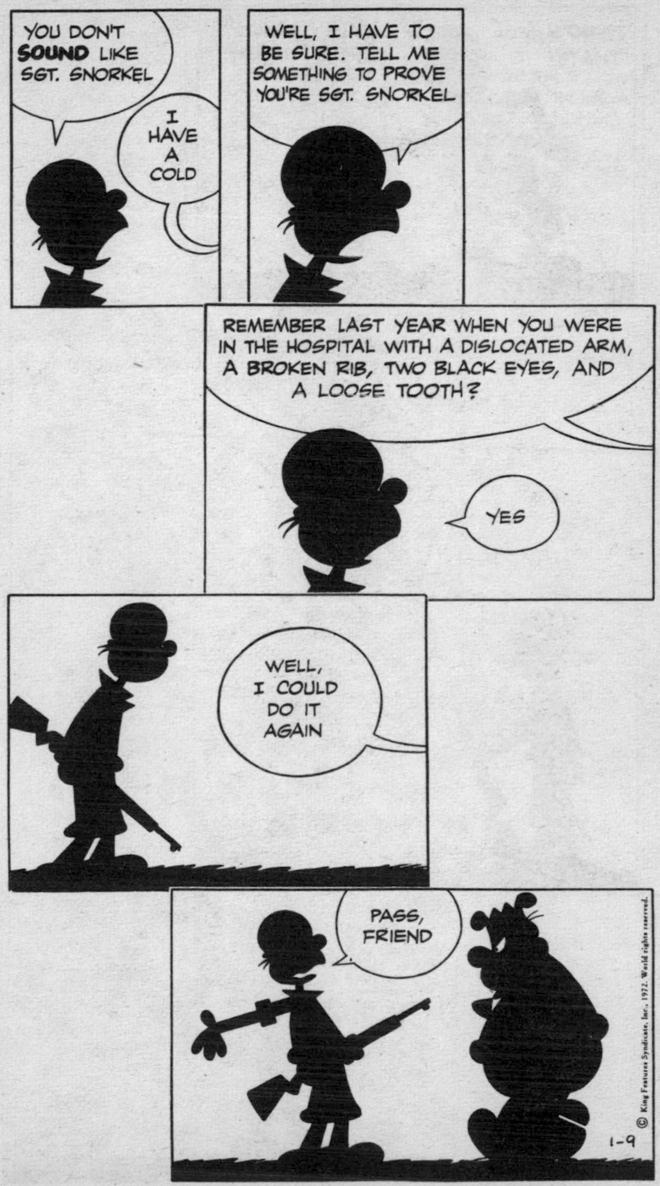
YOU DON'T **SOUND** LIKE SGT. SNORKEL
I HAVE A COLD
WELL, I HAVE TO BE SURE. TELL ME SOMETHING TO PROVE YOU'RE SGT. SNORKEL
REMEMBER LAST YEAR WHEN YOU WERE IN THE HOSPITAL WITH A DISLOCATED ARM, A BROKEN RIB, TWO BLACK EYES, AND A LOOSE TOOTH?
YES
WELL, I COULD DO IT AGAIN
PASS, FRIEND
1-9
© King Features Syndicate, Inc., 1972. World rights reserved.

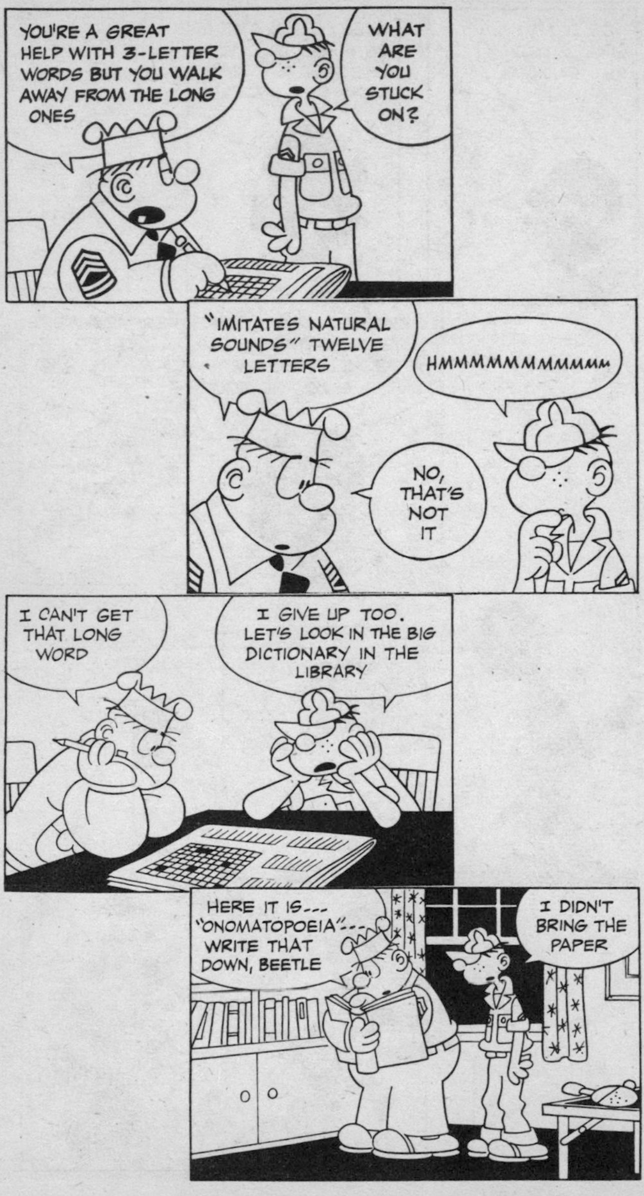
YOU'RE A GREAT HELP WITH 3-LETTER WORDS BUT YOU WALK AWAY FROM THE LONG ONES
WHAT ARE YOU STUCK ON?
"IMITATES NATURAL SOUNDS" TWELVE LETTERS
HMMMMMMMMMMM
NO, THAT'S NOT IT
I CAN'T GET THAT LONG WORD
I GIVE UP TOO. LET'S LOOK IN THE BIG DICTIONARY IN THE LIBRARY
HERE IT IS--- "ONOMATOPOEIA"--- WRITE THAT DOWN, BEETLE
I DIDN'T BRING THE PAPER

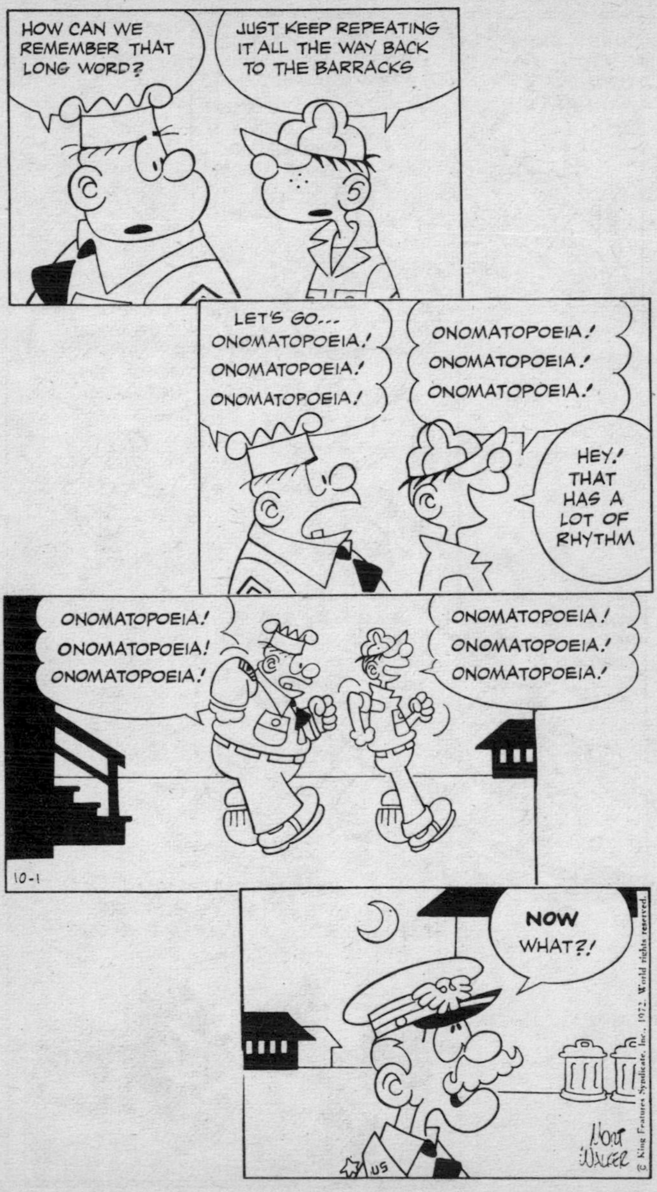
HOW CAN WE REMEMBER THAT LONG WORD?
JUST KEEP REPEATING IT ALL THE WAY BACK TO THE BARRACKS
LET'S GO... ONOMATOPOEIA! ONOMATOPOEIA! ONOMATOPOEIA!
ONOMATOPOEIA! ONOMATOPOEIA! ONOMATOPOEIA!
HEY! THAT HAS A LOT OF RHYTHM
ONOMATOPOEIA! ONOMATOPOEIA! ONOMATOPOEIA!
ONOMATOPOEIA! ONOMATOPOEIA! ONOMATOPOEIA!
10-1
NOW WHAT?!
US
© King Features Syndicate, Inc., 1972. World rights reserved.

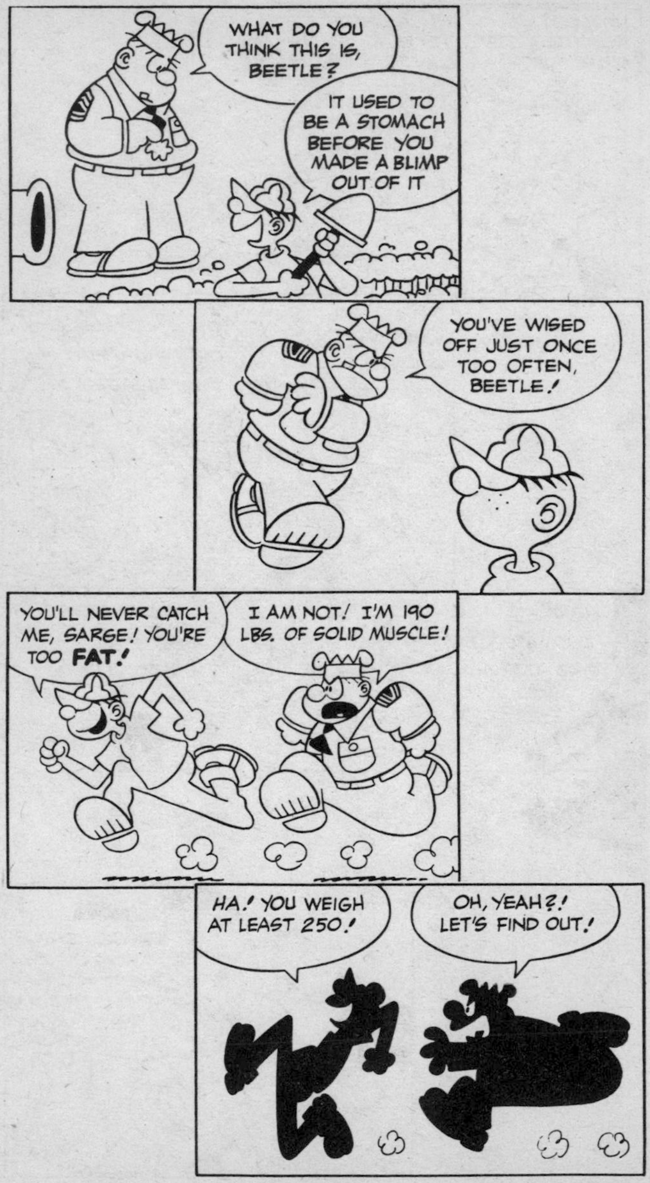

WHAT DO YOU THINK THIS IS, BEETLE?
IT USED TO BE A STOMACH BEFORE YOU MADE A BLIMP OUT OF IT
YOU'VE WISED OFF JUST ONCE TOO OFTEN, BEETLE!
YOU'LL NEVER CATCH ME, SARGE! YOU'RE TOO FAT!
I AM NOT! I'M 190 LBS. OF SOLID MUSCLE!
HA! YOU WEIGH AT LEAST 250!
OH, YEAH?! LET'S FIND OUT!

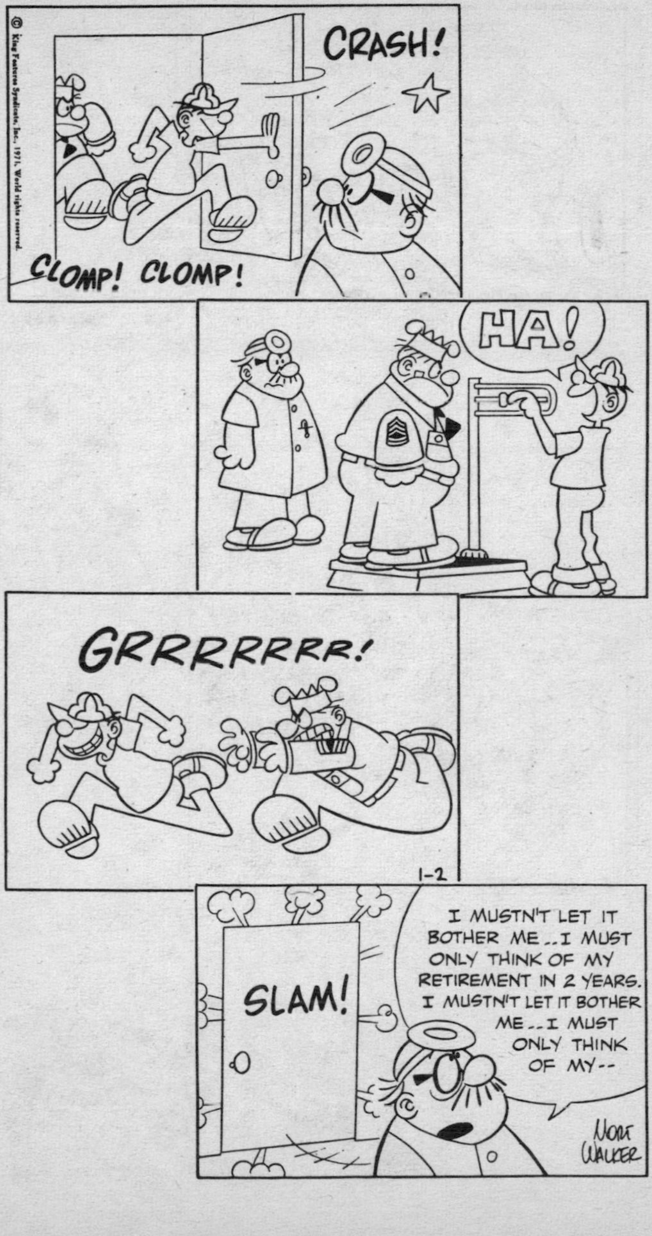
© King Features Syndicate, Inc., 1971. World rights reserved.
CRASH!
CLOMP! CLOMP!
HA!
GRRRRRRR!
1-2
SLAM!
I MUSTN'T LET IT BOTHER ME..I MUST ONLY THINK OF MY RETIREMENT IN 2 YEARS. I MUSTN'T LET IT BOTHER ME..I MUST ONLY THINK OF MY--
MORT WALKER

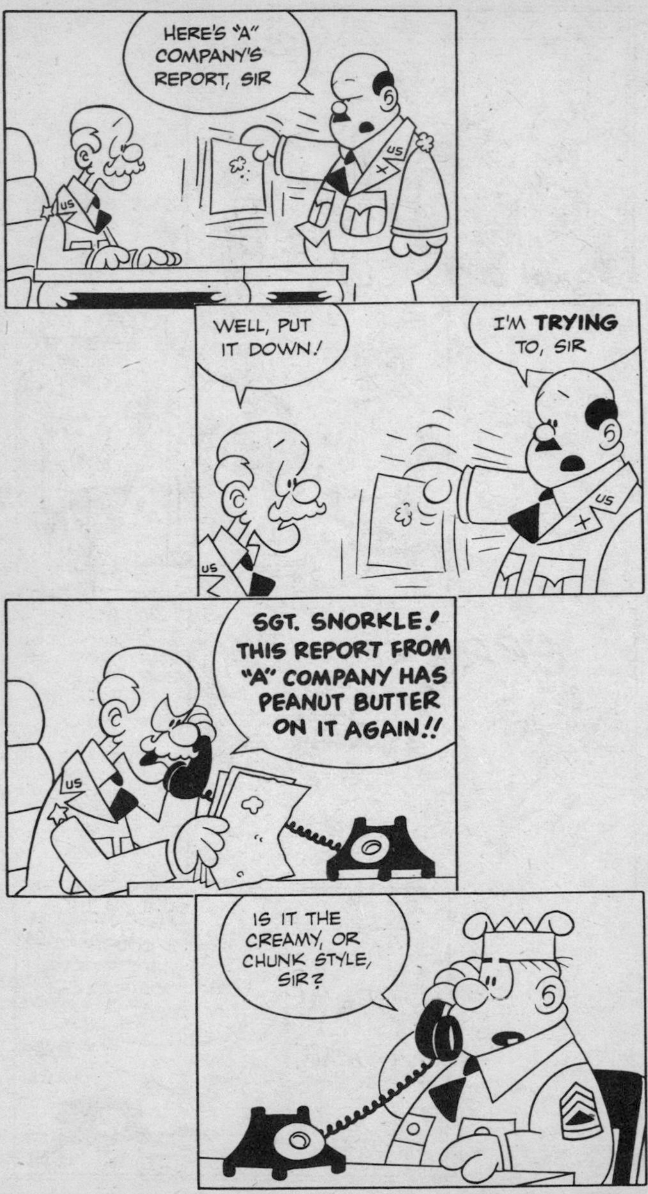
HERE'S "A" COMPANY'S REPORT, SIR
WELL, PUT IT DOWN!
I'M **TRYING** TO, SIR
SGT. SNORKLE! THIS REPORT FROM "A" COMPANY HAS PEANUT BUTTER ON IT AGAIN!!
IS IT THE CREAMY, OR CHUNK STYLE, SIR?

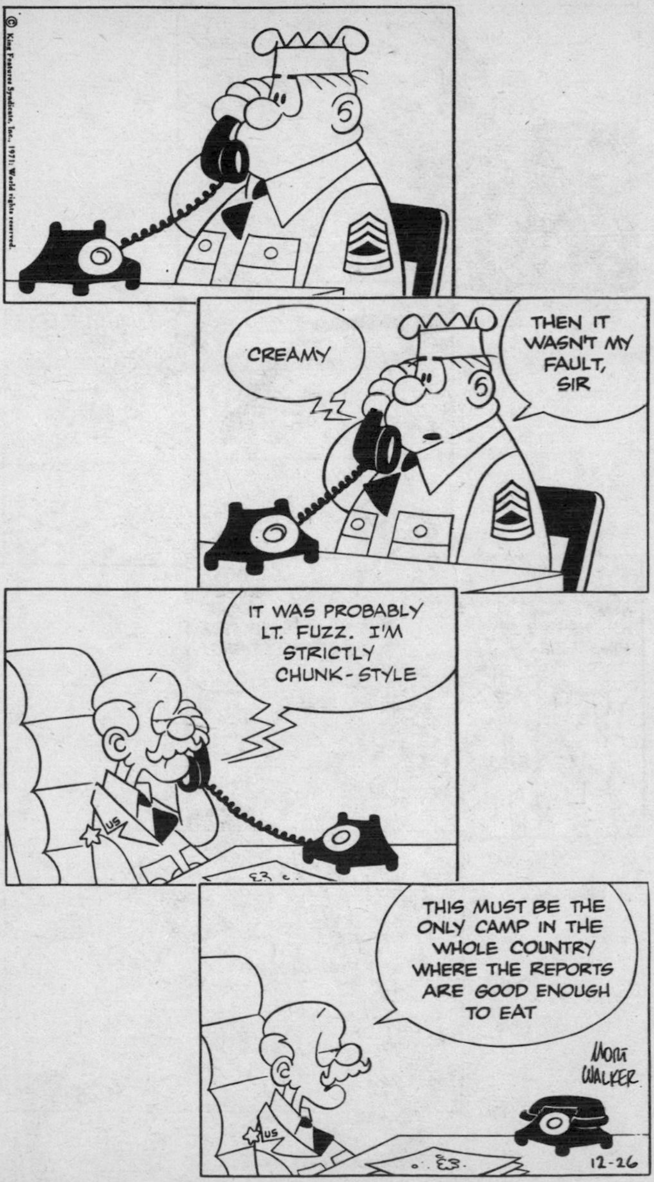
© King Features Syndicate, Inc., 1971. World rights reserved.
CREAMY
THEN IT WASN'T MY FAULT, SIR
IT WAS PROBABLY LT. FUZZ. I'M STRICTLY CHUNK-STYLE
THIS MUST BE THE ONLY CAMP IN THE WHOLE COUNTRY WHERE THE REPORTS ARE GOOD ENOUGH TO EAT
MORT WALKER
12-26

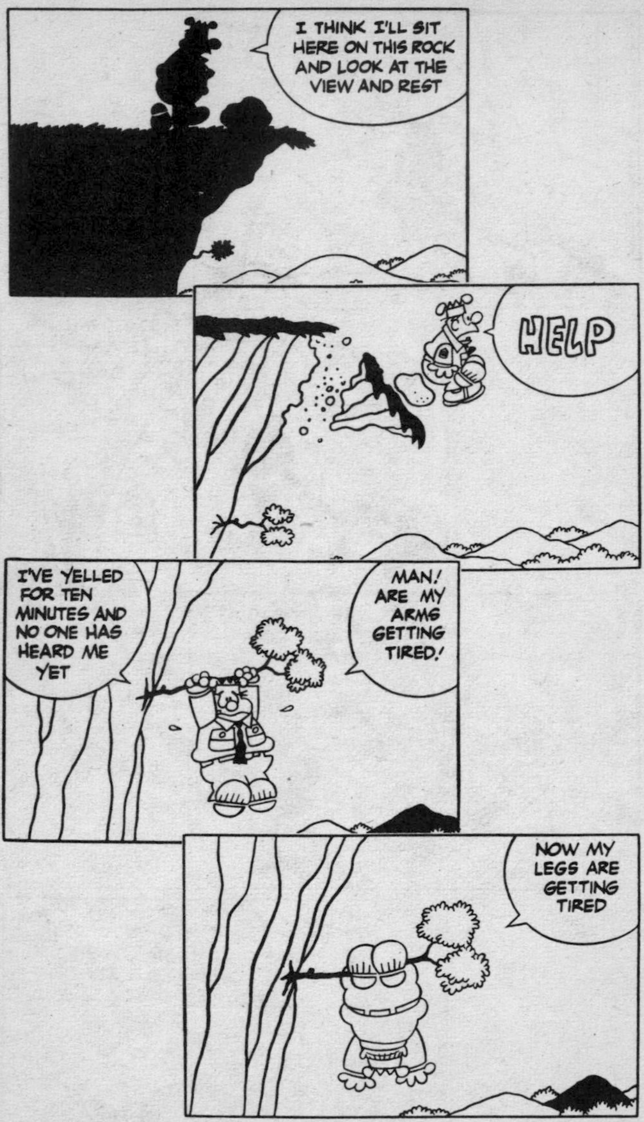
I THINK I'LL SIT HERE ON THIS ROCK AND LOOK AT THE VIEW AND REST
HELP
I'VE YELLED FOR TEN MINUTES AND NO ONE HAS HEARD ME YET
MAN! ARE MY ARMS GETTING TIRED!
NOW MY LEGS ARE GETTING TIRED

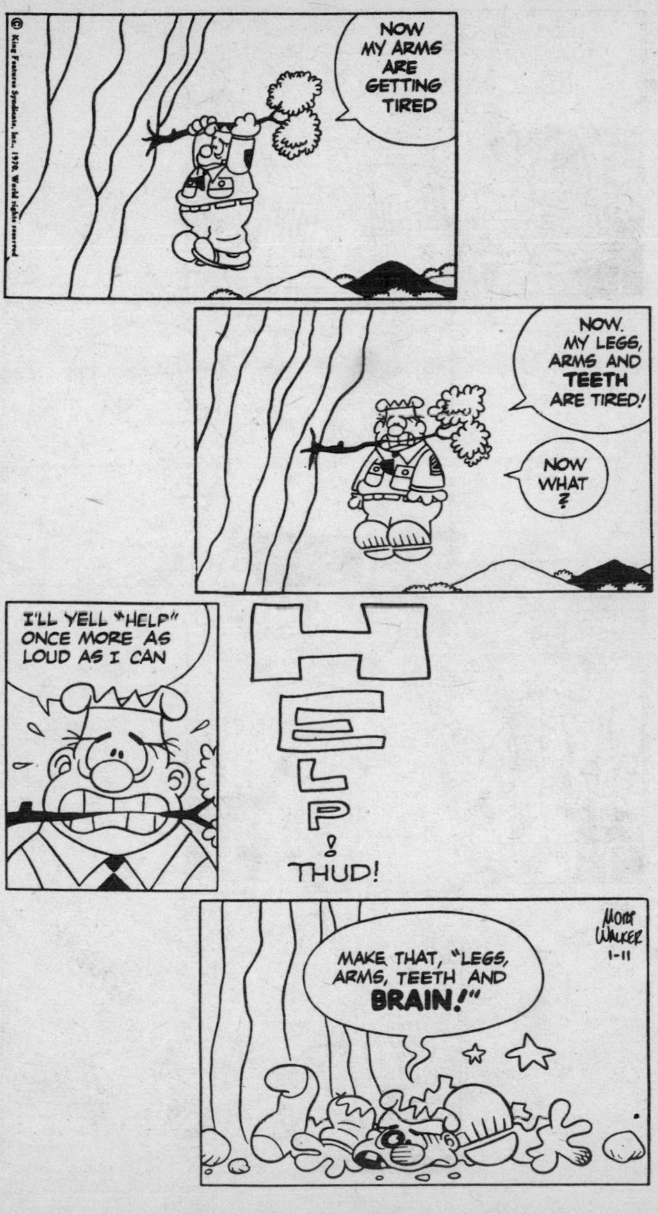
© King Features Syndicate, Inc., 1978. World rights reserved
NOW MY ARMS ARE GETTING TIRED
NOW. MY LEGS, ARMS AND TEETH ARE TIRED!
NOW WHAT?
I'LL YELL "HELP" ONCE MORE AS LOUD AS I CAN
HELP!
THUD!
MAKE THAT, "LEGS, ARMS, TEETH AND BRAIN!"
MORT WALKER
1-11

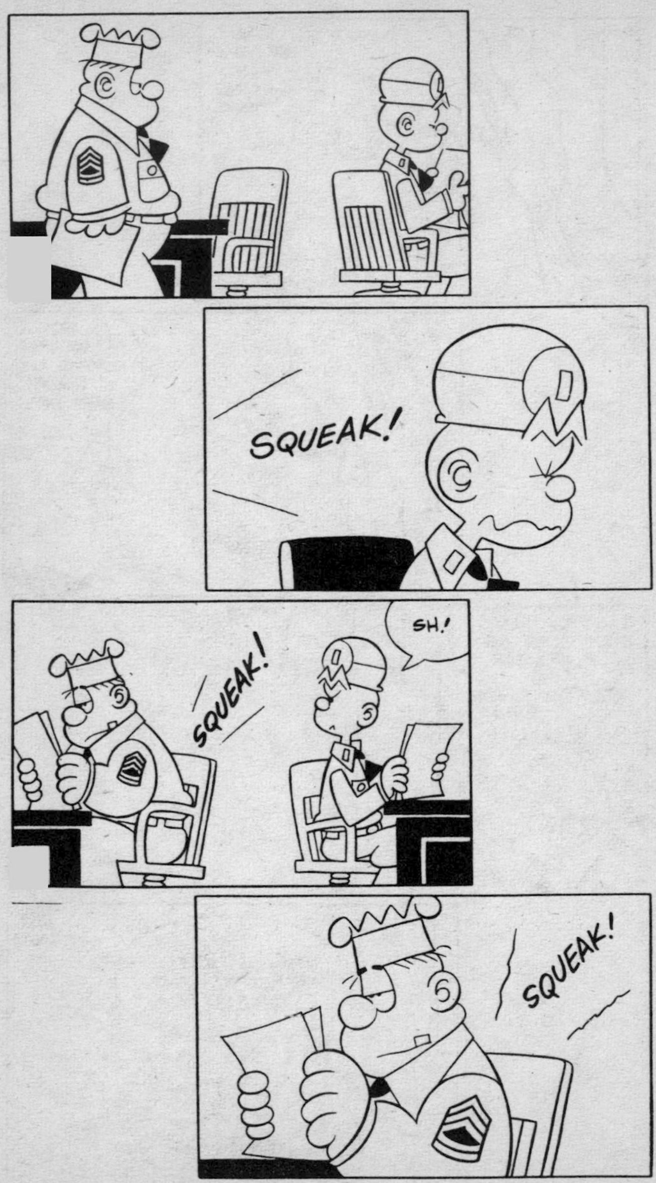
SQUEAK!
SQUEAK!
SH!
SQUEAK!

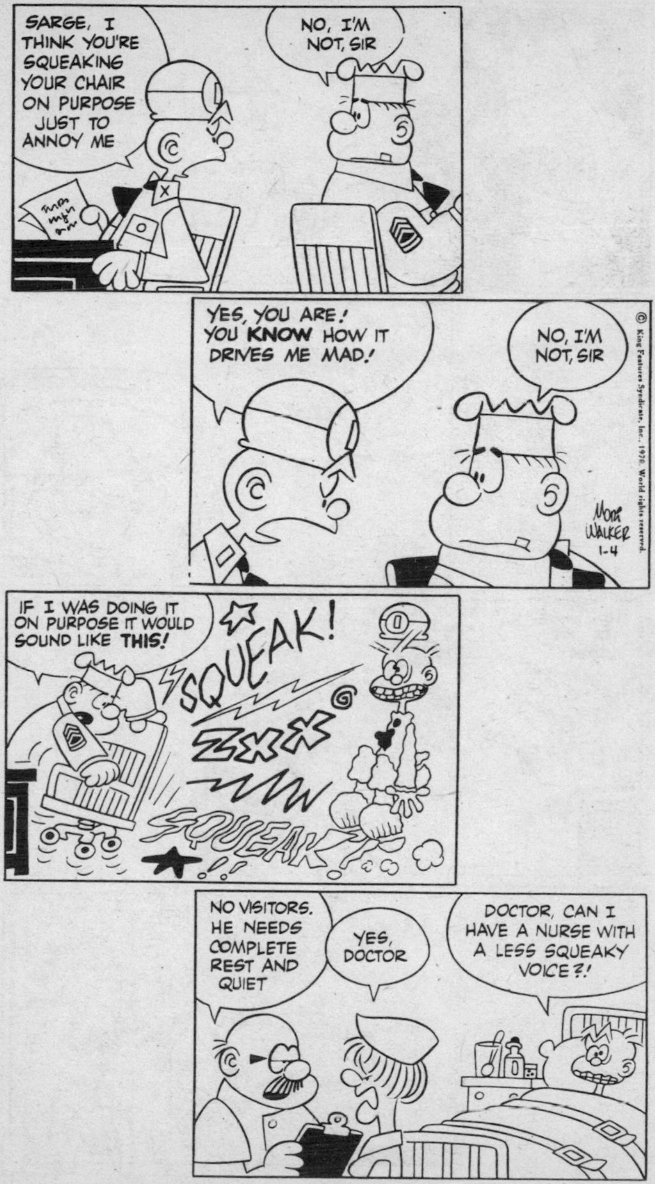
SARGE, I THINK YOU'RE SQUEAKING YOUR CHAIR ON PURPOSE JUST TO ANNOY ME
NO, I'M NOT, SIR
YES, YOU ARE! YOU **KNOW** HOW IT DRIVES ME MAD!
NO, I'M NOT, SIR
MORT WALKER 1-4
IF I WAS DOING IT ON PURPOSE IT WOULD SOUND LIKE **THIS**!
SQUEAK!
SQUEAK!
NO VISITORS. HE NEEDS COMPLETE REST AND QUIET
YES, DOCTOR
DOCTOR, CAN I HAVE A NURSE WITH A LESS SQUEAKY VOICE?!

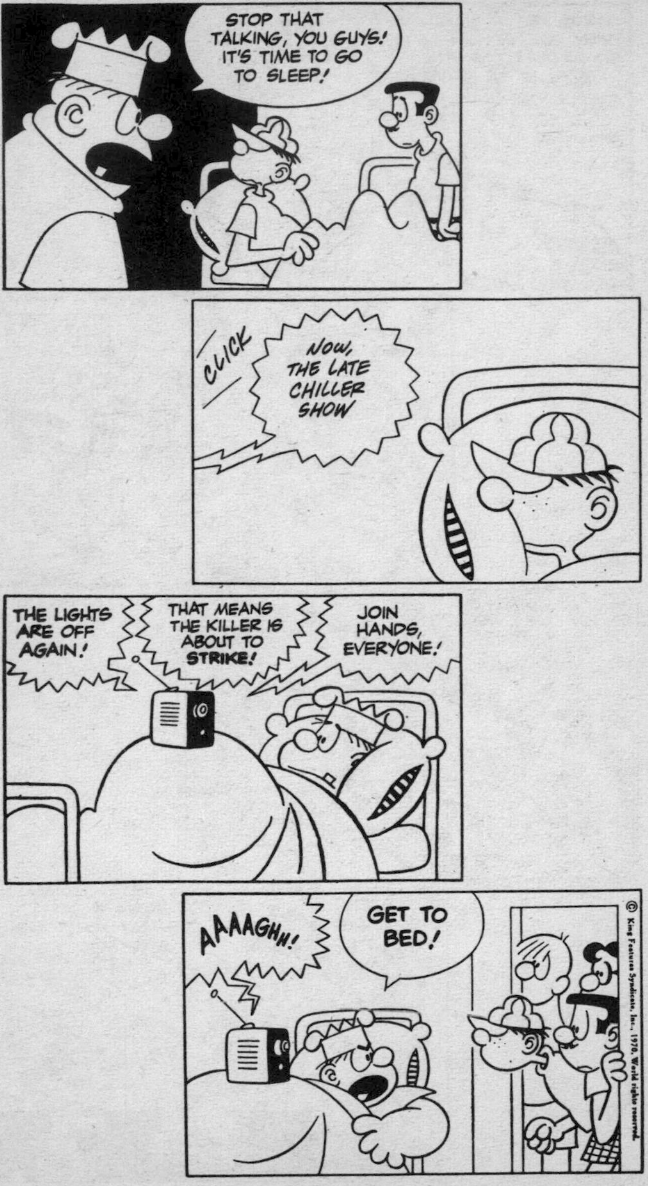
STOP THAT TALKING, YOU GUYS! IT'S TIME TO GO TO SLEEP!
CLICK
NOW, THE LATE CHILLER SHOW
THE LIGHTS ARE OFF AGAIN!
THAT MEANS THE KILLER IS ABOUT TO STRIKE!
JOIN HANDS, EVERYONE!
AAAAGHH!
GET TO BED!

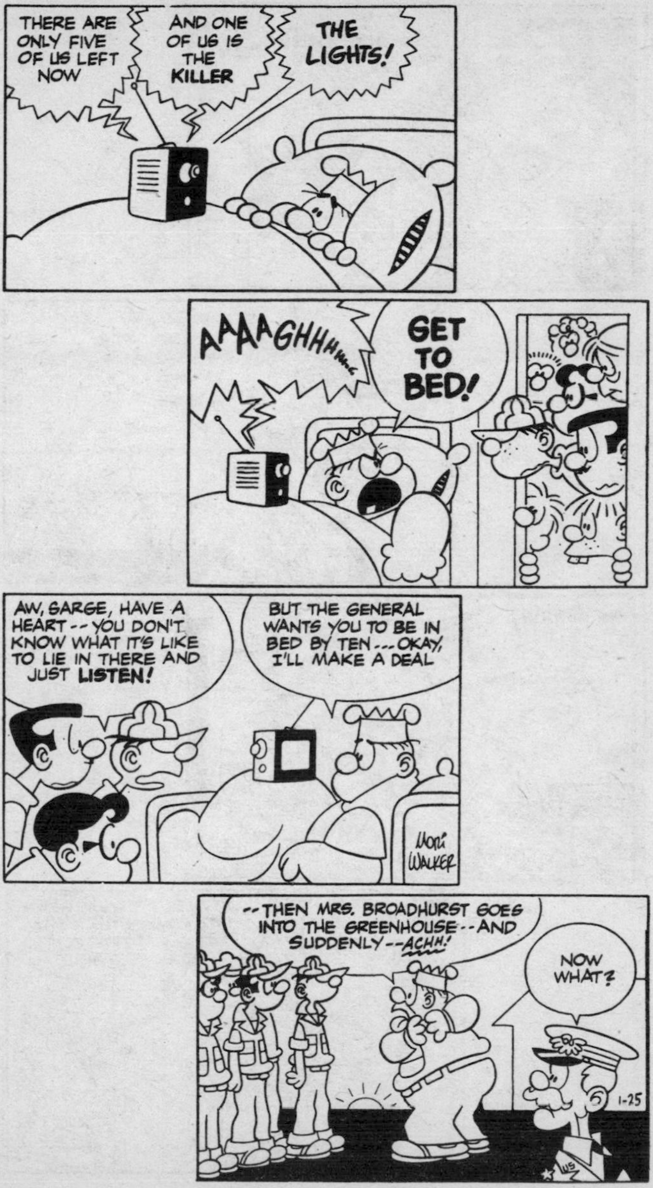
THERE ARE ONLY FIVE OF US LEFT NOW
AND ONE OF US IS THE KILLER
THE LIGHTS!
AAAAGHHH...
GET TO BED!
AW, SARGE, HAVE A HEART -- YOU DON'T KNOW WHAT IT'S LIKE TO LIE IN THERE AND JUST LISTEN!
BUT THE GENERAL WANTS YOU TO BE IN BED BY TEN --- OKAY, I'LL MAKE A DEAL
MORT WALKER
-- THEN MRS. BROADHURST GOES INTO THE GREENHOUSE -- AND SUDDENLY -- ACHH!
NOW WHAT?
1-25

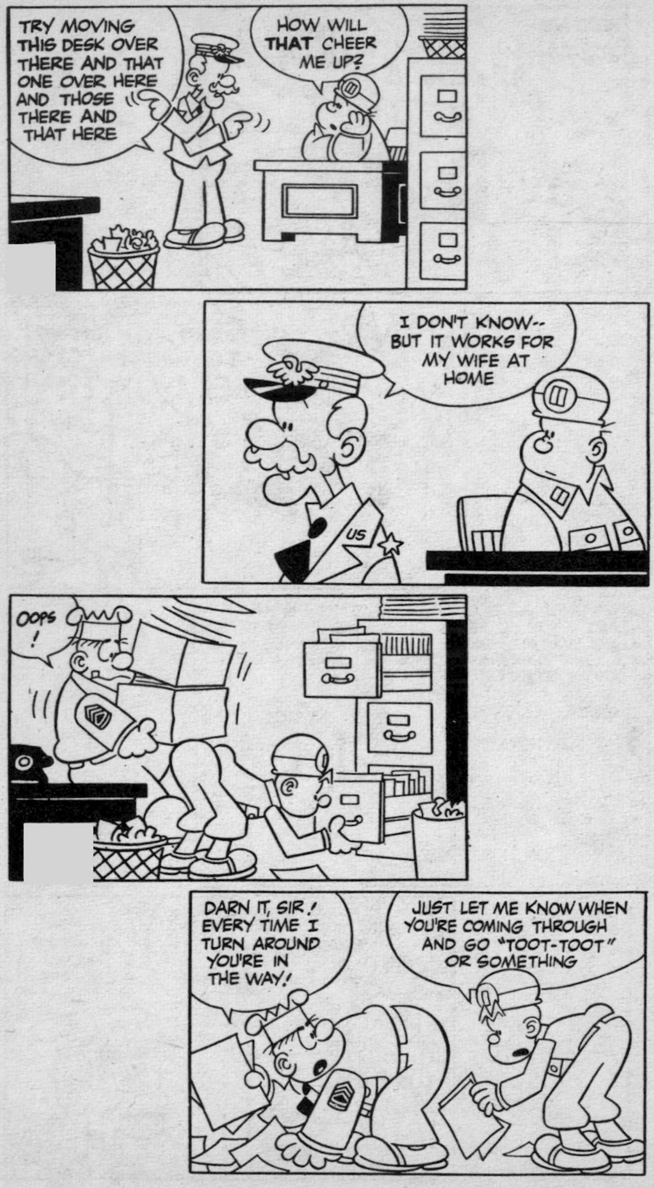

TRY MOVING THIS DESK OVER THERE AND THAT ONE OVER HERE AND THOSE THERE AND THAT HERE
HOW WILL **THAT** CHEER ME UP?
I DON'T KNOW-- BUT IT WORKS FOR MY WIFE AT HOME
OOPS!
DARN IT, SIR! EVERY TIME I TURN AROUND YOU'RE IN THE WAY!
JUST LET ME KNOW WHEN YOU'RE COMING THROUGH AND GO "TOOT-TOOT" OR SOMETHING

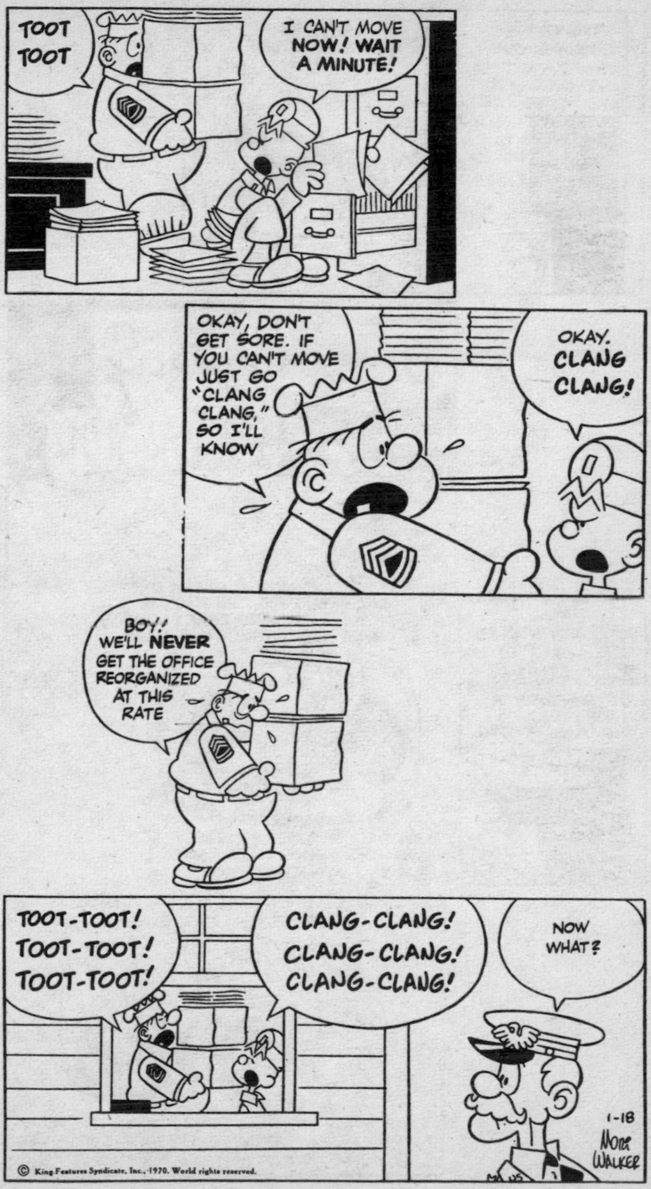
TOOT TOOT
I CAN'T MOVE NOW! WAIT A MINUTE!
OKAY, DON'T GET SORE. IF YOU CAN'T MOVE JUST GO "CLANG CLANG," SO I'LL KNOW
OKAY. CLANG CLANG!
BOY! WE'LL NEVER GET THE OFFICE REORGANIZED AT THIS RATE
TOOT-TOOT! TOOT-TOOT! TOOT-TOOT!
CLANG-CLANG! CLANG-CLANG! CLANG-CLANG!
NOW WHAT?
1-18
MORT WALKER
© King Features Syndicate, Inc., 1970. World rights reserved.

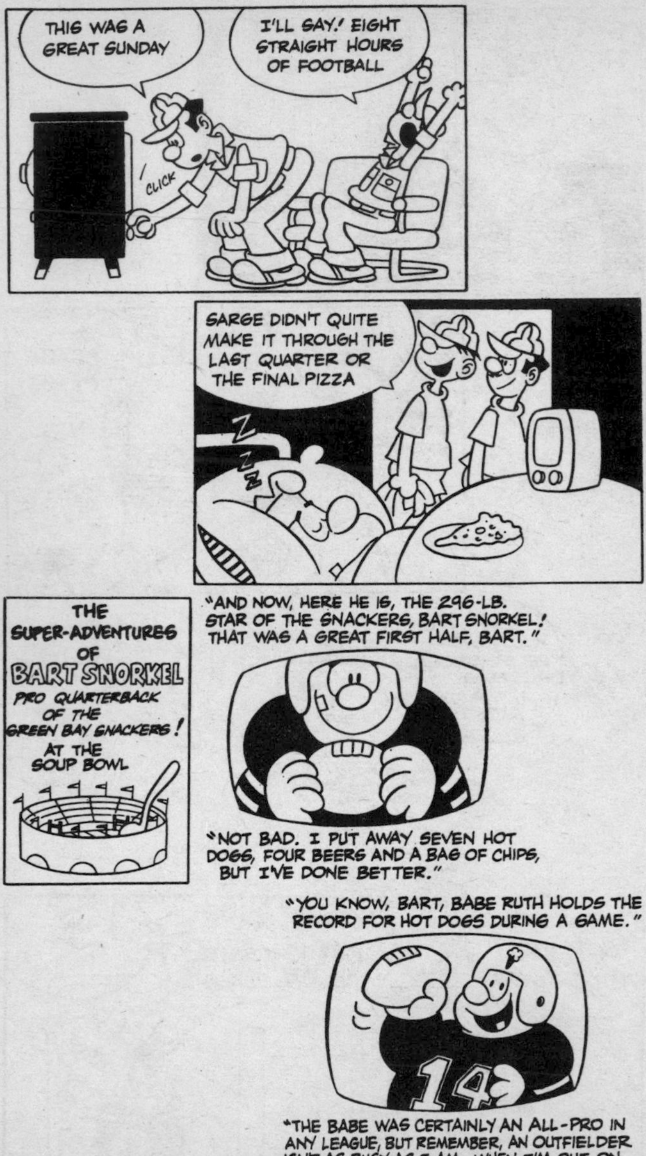
THIS WAS A GREAT SUNDAY
I'LL SAY! EIGHT STRAIGHT HOURS OF FOOTBALL
CLICK
SARGE DIDN'T QUITE MAKE IT THROUGH THE LAST QUARTER OR THE FINAL PIZZA
Z Z Z
THE SUPER-ADVENTURES OF BART SNORKEL PRO QUARTERBACK OF THE GREEN BAY SNACKERS! AT THE SOUP BOWL
"AND NOW, HERE HE IS, THE 296-LB. STAR OF THE SNACKERS, BART SNORKEL! THAT WAS A GREAT FIRST HALF, BART."
"NOT BAD. I PUT AWAY SEVEN HOT DOGS, FOUR BEERS AND A BAG OF CHIPS, BUT I'VE DONE BETTER."
"YOU KNOW, BART, BABE RUTH HOLDS THE RECORD FOR HOT DOGS DURING A GAME."
14
"THE BABE WAS CERTAINLY AN ALL-PRO IN ANY LEAGUE, BUT REMEMBER, AN OUTFIELDER ISN'T AS BUSY AS I AM. WHEN I'M OUT ON THE FIELD I'VE ONLY GOT ONE HAND FREE."

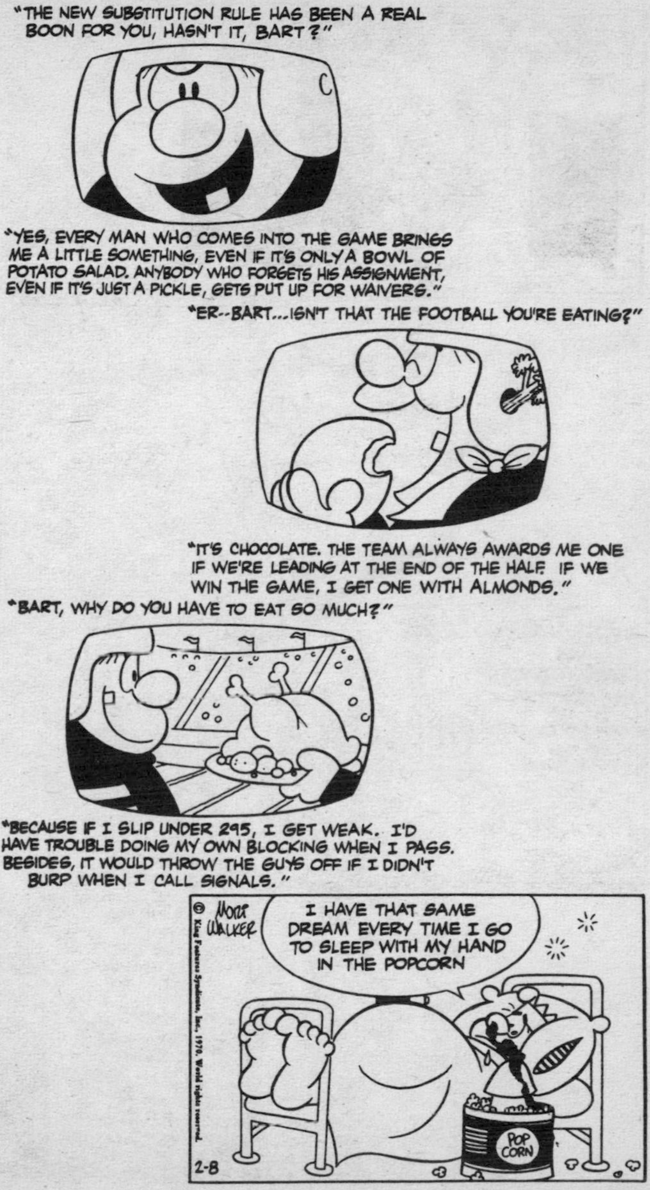
"THE NEW SUBSTITUTION RULE HAS BEEN A REAL BOON FOR YOU, HASN'T IT, BART?"
"YES, EVERY MAN WHO COMES INTO THE GAME BRINGS ME A LITTLE SOMETHING, EVEN IF IT'S ONLY A BOWL OF POTATO SALAD. ANYBODY WHO FORGETS HIS ASSIGNMENT, EVEN IF IT'S JUST A PICKLE, GETS PUT UP FOR WAIVERS."
"ER--BART... ISN'T THAT THE FOOTBALL YOU'RE EATING?"
"IT'S CHOCOLATE. THE TEAM ALWAYS AWARDS ME ONE IF WE'RE LEADING AT THE END OF THE HALF. IF WE WIN THE GAME, I GET ONE WITH ALMONDS."
"BART, WHY DO YOU HAVE TO EAT SO MUCH?"
"BECAUSE IF I SLIP UNDER 295, I GET WEAK. I'D HAVE TROUBLE DOING MY OWN BLOCKING WHEN I PASS. BESIDES, IT WOULD THROW THE GUYS OFF IF I DIDN'T BURP WHEN I CALL SIGNALS."
MORT WALKER
© King Features Syndicate, Inc., 1970. World rights reserved.
I HAVE THAT SAME DREAM EVERY TIME I GO TO SLEEP WITH MY HAND IN THE POPCORN
POP CORN
2-8

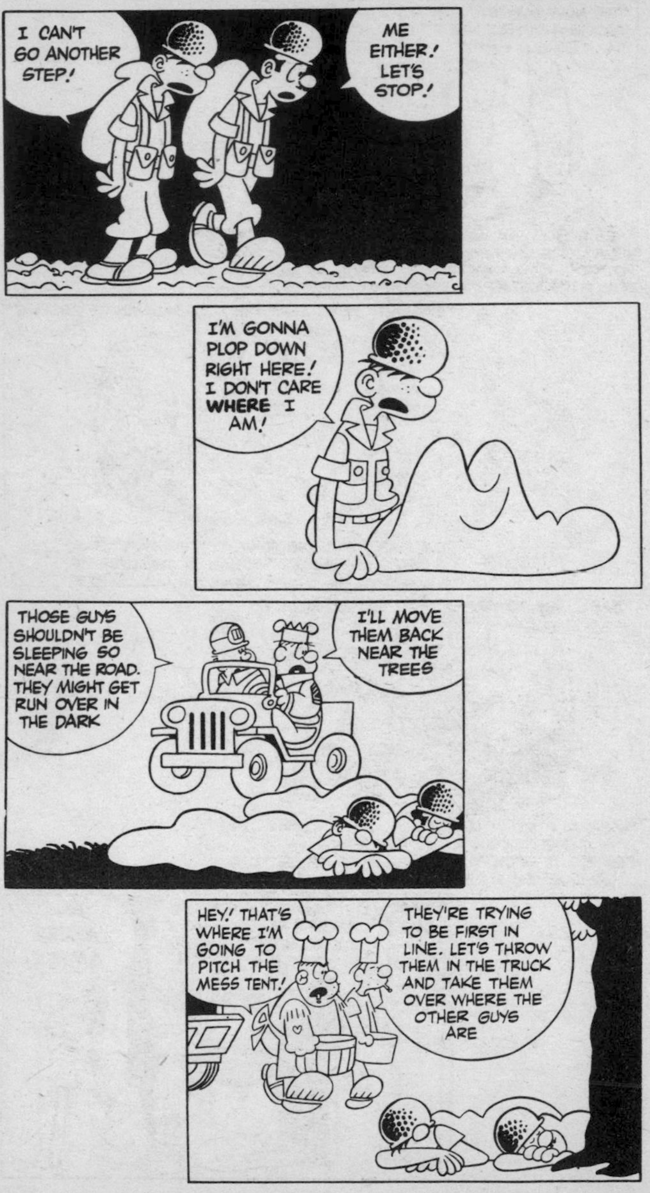
I CAN'T GO ANOTHER STEP!
ME EITHER! LET'S STOP!
I'M GONNA PLOP DOWN RIGHT HERE! I DON'T CARE **WHERE** I AM!
THOSE GUYS SHOULDN'T BE SLEEPING SO NEAR THE ROAD. THEY MIGHT GET RUN OVER IN THE DARK
I'LL MOVE THEM BACK NEAR THE TREES
HEY! THAT'S WHERE I'M GOING TO PITCH THE MESS TENT!
THEY'RE TRYING TO BE FIRST IN LINE. LET'S THROW THEM IN THE TRUCK AND TAKE THEM OVER WHERE THE OTHER GUYS ARE

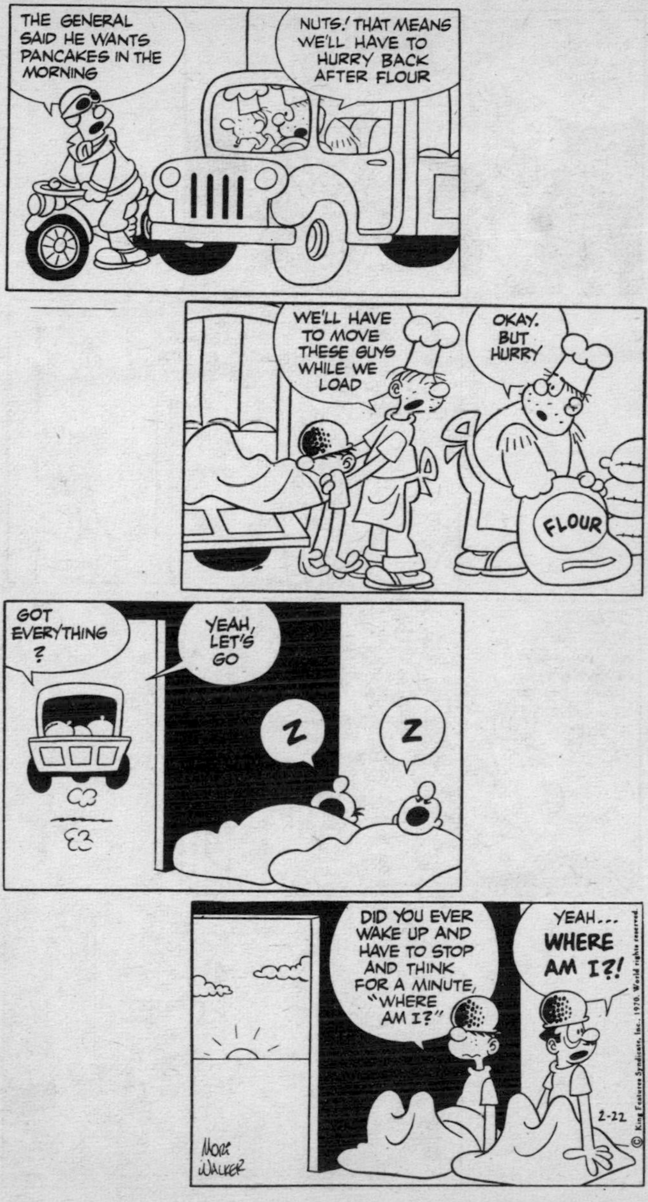
THE GENERAL SAID HE WANTS PANCAKES IN THE MORNING
NUTS! THAT MEANS WE'LL HAVE TO HURRY BACK AFTER FLOUR
WE'LL HAVE TO MOVE THESE GUYS WHILE WE LOAD
OKAY. BUT HURRY
FLOUR
GOT EVERYTHING ?
YEAH, LET'S GO
Z
Z
DID YOU EVER WAKE UP AND HAVE TO STOP AND THINK FOR A MINUTE, "WHERE AM I?"
YEAH... WHERE AM I?!
MORT WALKER
2-22
© King Features Syndicate, Inc., 1970. World rights reserved.

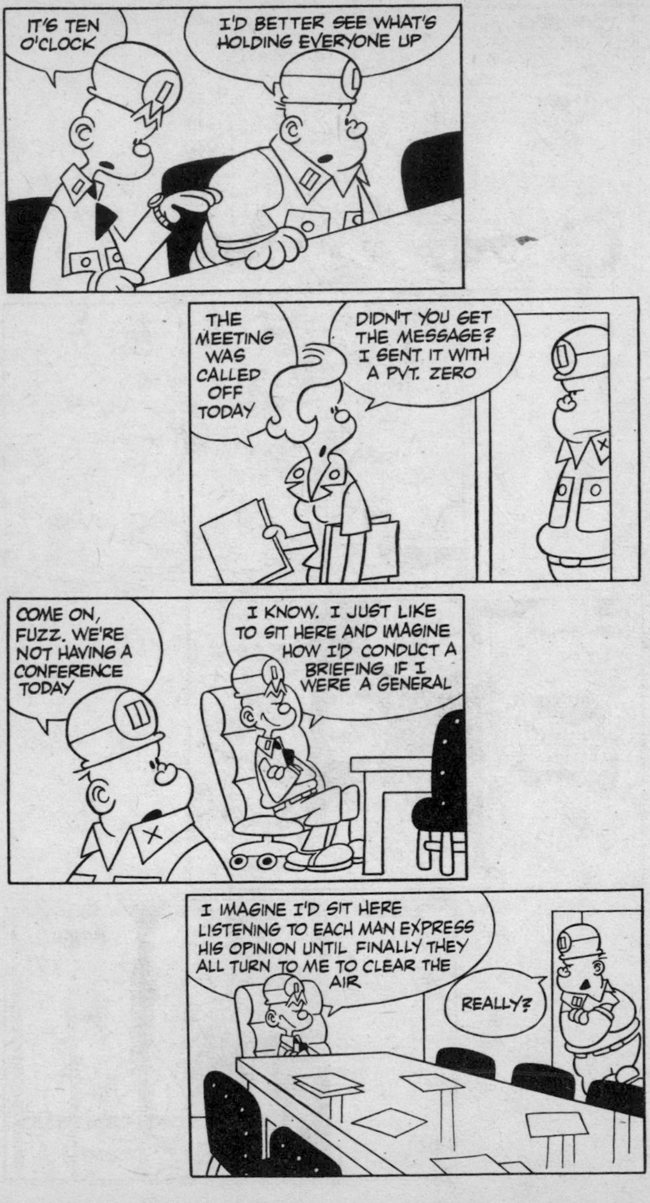
IT'S TEN O'CLOCK
I'D BETTER SEE WHAT'S HOLDING EVERYONE UP
THE MEETING WAS CALLED OFF TODAY
DIDN'T YOU GET THE MESSAGE? I SENT IT WITH A PVT. ZERO
COME ON, FUZZ. WE'RE NOT HAVING A CONFERENCE TODAY
I KNOW. I JUST LIKE TO SIT HERE AND IMAGINE HOW I'D CONDUCT A BRIEFING IF I WERE A GENERAL
I IMAGINE I'D SIT HERE LISTENING TO EACH MAN EXPRESS HIS OPINION UNTIL FINALLY THEY ALL TURN TO ME TO CLEAR THE AIR
REALLY?

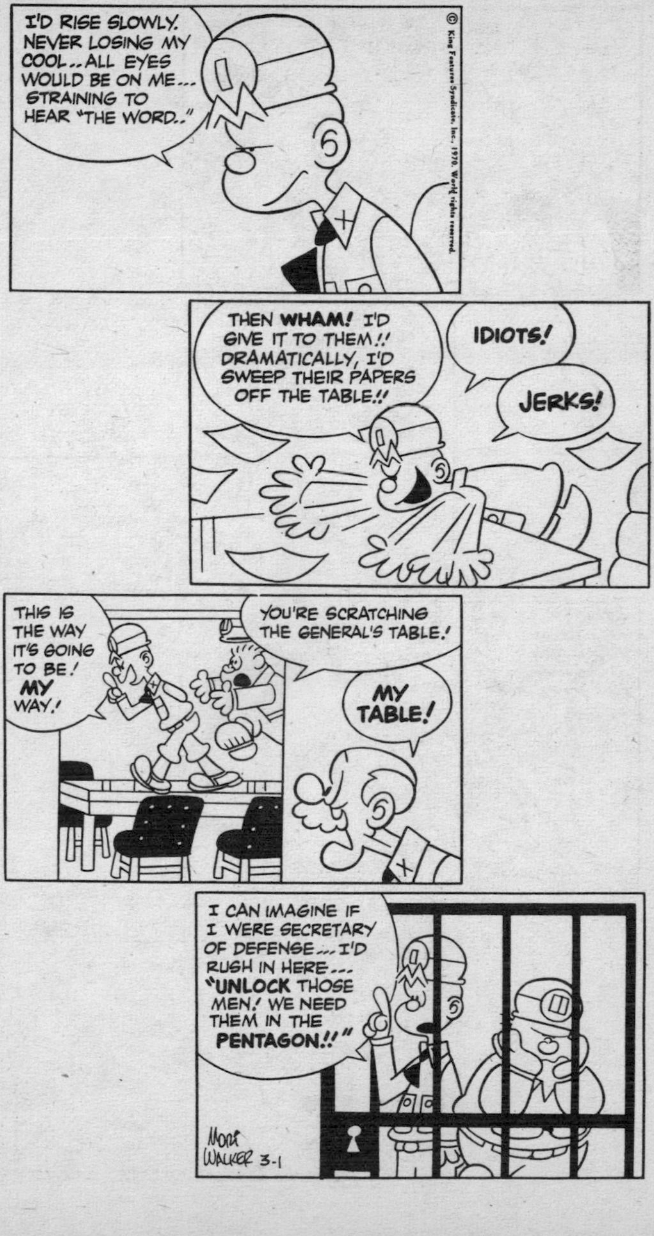
I'D RISE SLOWLY. NEVER LOSING MY COOL.. ALL EYES WOULD BE ON ME... STRAINING TO HEAR "THE WORD.."
© King Features Syndicate, Inc., 1970. World rights reserved.
THEN WHAM! I'D GIVE IT TO THEM!! DRAMATICALLY, I'D SWEEP THEIR PAPERS OFF THE TABLE!!
IDIOTS!
JERKS!
THIS IS THE WAY IT'S GOING TO BE! MY WAY!
YOU'RE SCRATCHING THE GENERAL'S TABLE!
MY TABLE!
I CAN IMAGINE IF I WERE SECRETARY OF DEFENSE... I'D RUSH IN HERE... "UNLOCK THOSE MEN! WE NEED THEM IN THE PENTAGON!!"
MORT WALKER 3-1

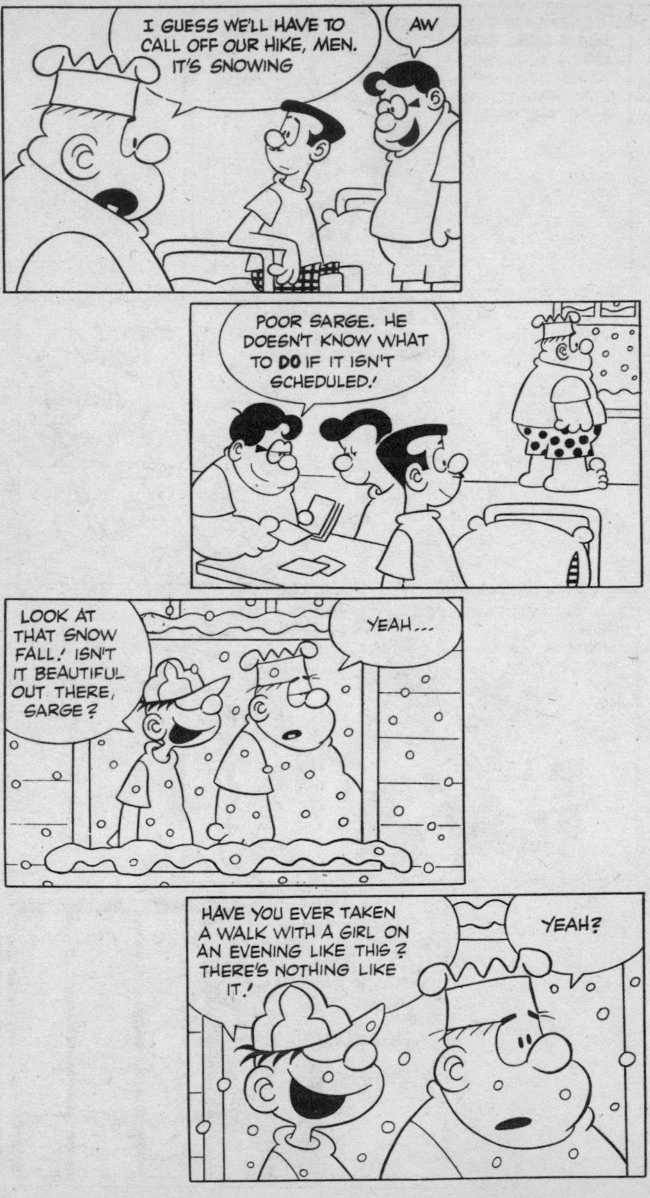

I GUESS WE'LL HAVE TO CALL OFF OUR HIKE, MEN. IT'S SNOWING
AW
POOR SARGE. HE DOESN'T KNOW WHAT TO DO IF IT ISN'T SCHEDULED!
LOOK AT THAT SNOW FALL! ISN'T IT BEAUTIFUL OUT THERE, SARGE?
YEAH...
HAVE YOU EVER TAKEN A WALK WITH A GIRL ON AN EVENING LIKE THIS? THERE'S NOTHING LIKE IT!
YEAH?

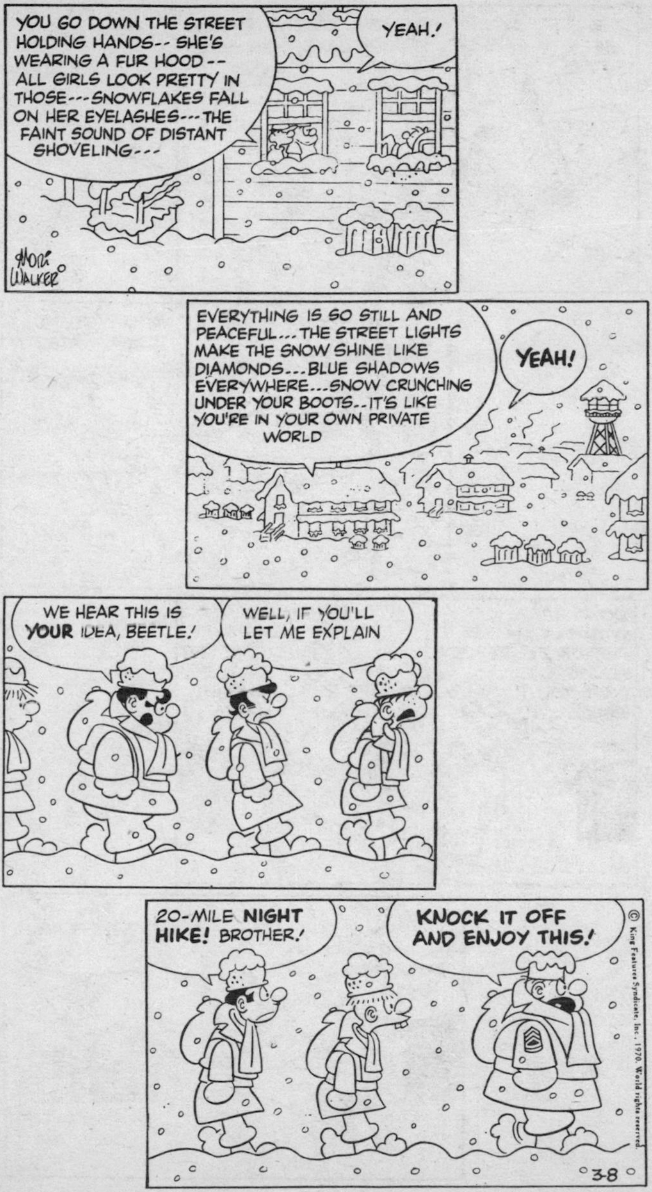
YOU GO DOWN THE STREET HOLDING HANDS-- SHE'S WEARING A FUR HOOD-- ALL GIRLS LOOK PRETTY IN THOSE---SNOWFLAKES FALL ON HER EYELASHES---THE FAINT SOUND OF DISTANT SHOVELING---
YEAH!
MORT WALKER
EVERYTHING IS SO STILL AND PEACEFUL...THE STREET LIGHTS MAKE THE SNOW SHINE LIKE DIAMONDS...BLUE SHADOWS EVERYWHERE...SNOW CRUNCHING UNDER YOUR BOOTS..IT'S LIKE YOU'RE IN YOUR OWN PRIVATE WORLD
YEAH!
WE HEAR THIS IS YOUR IDEA, BEETLE!
WELL, IF YOU'LL LET ME EXPLAIN
20-MILE NIGHT HIKE! BROTHER!
KNOCK IT OFF AND ENJOY THIS!
3-8

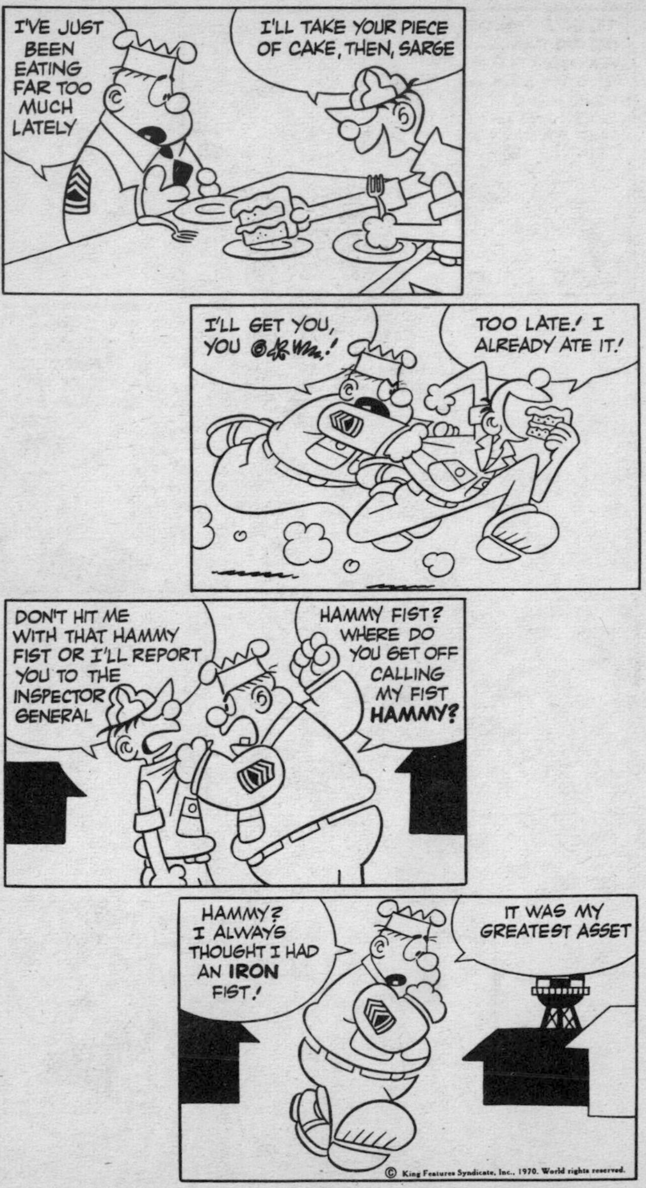
I'VE JUST BEEN EATING FAR TOO MUCH LATELY
I'LL TAKE YOUR PIECE OF CAKE, THEN, SARGE
I'LL GET YOU, YOU
TOO LATE! I ALREADY ATE IT!
DON'T HIT ME WITH THAT HAMMY FIST OR I'LL REPORT YOU TO THE INSPECTOR GENERAL
HAMMY FIST? WHERE DO YOU GET OFF CALLING MY FIST HAMMY?
HAMMY? I ALWAYS THOUGHT I HAD AN IRON FIST!
IT WAS MY GREATEST ASSET
© King Features Syndicate, Inc., 1970. World rights reserved.

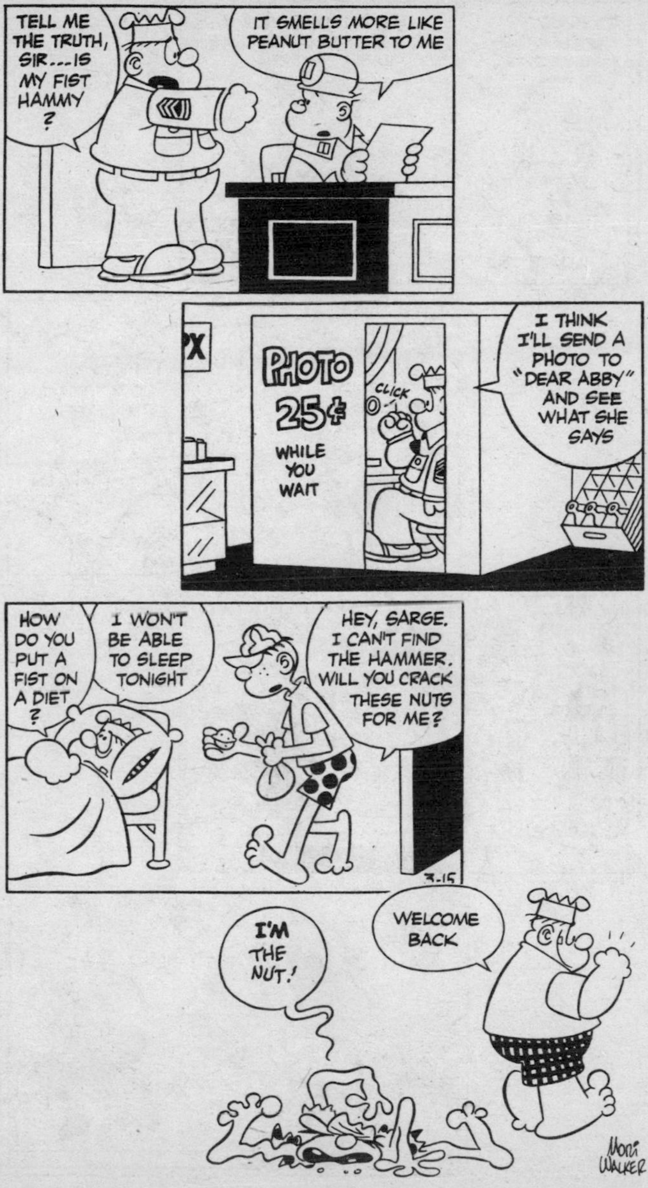
TELL ME THE TRUTH, SIR...IS MY FIST HAMMY ?
IT SMELLS MORE LIKE PEANUT BUTTER TO ME
PX
PHOTO 25¢ WHILE YOU WAIT
CLICK
I THINK I'LL SEND A PHOTO TO "DEAR ABBY" AND SEE WHAT SHE SAYS
HOW DO YOU PUT A FIST ON A DIET ?
I WON'T BE ABLE TO SLEEP TONIGHT
HEY, SARGE. I CAN'T FIND THE HAMMER. WILL YOU CRACK THESE NUTS FOR ME?
3-15
I'M THE NUT!
WELCOME BACK
MORT WALKER

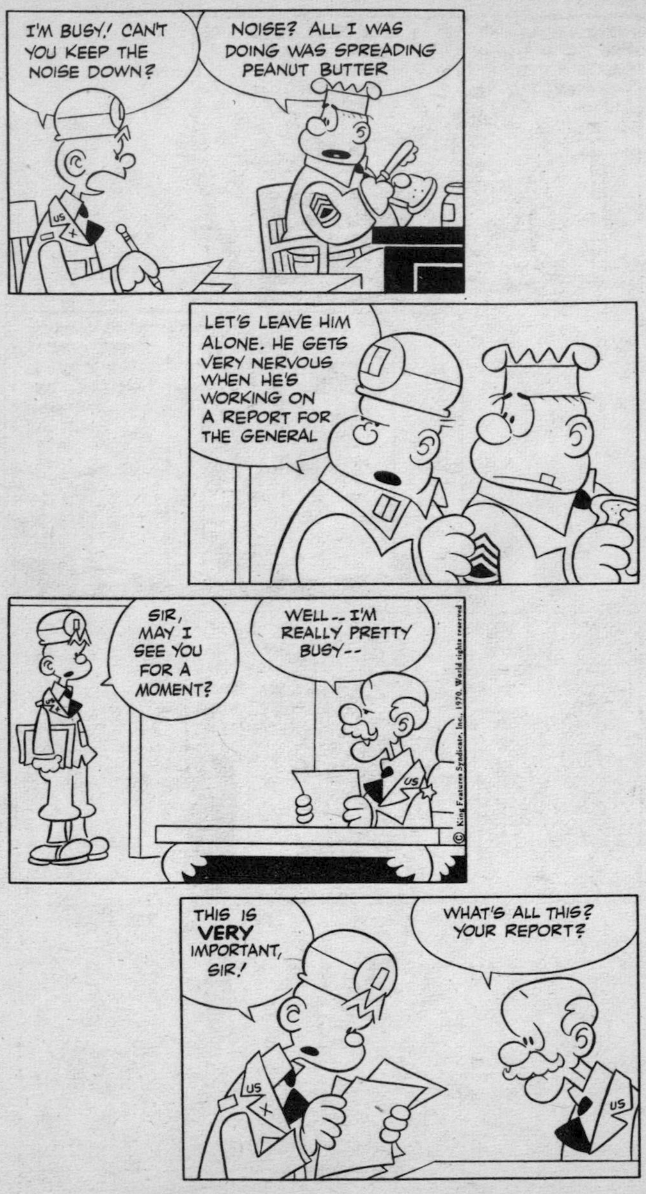
I'M BUSY! CAN'T YOU KEEP THE NOISE DOWN?
NOISE? ALL I WAS DOING WAS SPREADING PEANUT BUTTER
LET'S LEAVE HIM ALONE. HE GETS VERY NERVOUS WHEN HE'S WORKING ON A REPORT FOR THE GENERAL
SIR, MAY I SEE YOU FOR A MOMENT?
WELL-- I'M REALLY PRETTY BUSY--
© King Features Syndicate, Inc., 1970. World rights reserved
THIS IS **VERY** IMPORTANT, SIR!
WHAT'S ALL THIS? YOUR REPORT?

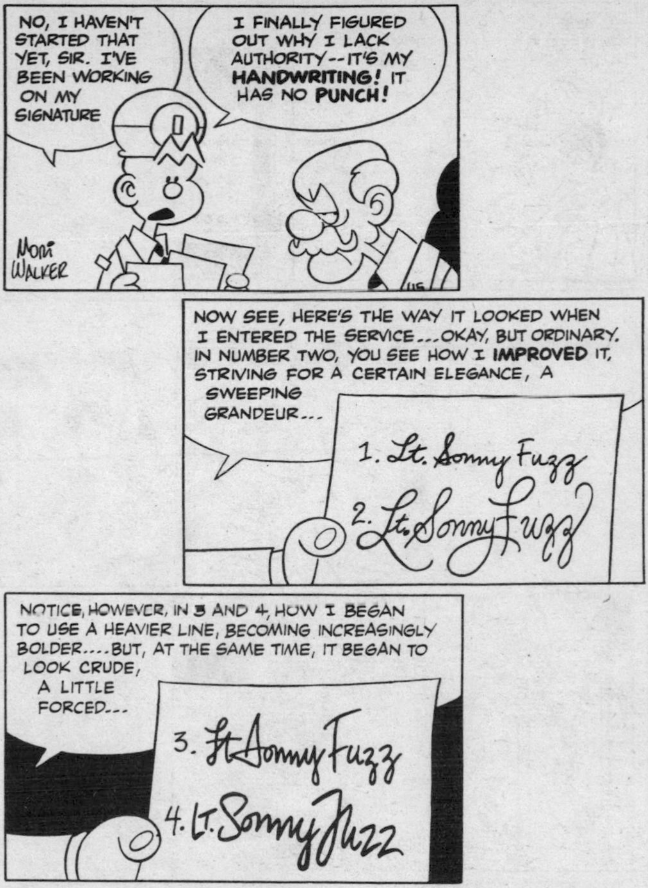
NO, I HAVEN'T STARTED THAT YET, SIR. I'VE BEEN WORKING ON MY SIGNATURE
I FINALLY FIGURED OUT WHY I LACK AUTHORITY--IT'S MY HANDWRITING! IT HAS NO PUNCH!
MORT WALKER
NOW SEE, HERE'S THE WAY IT LOOKED WHEN I ENTERED THE SERVICE...OKAY, BUT ORDINARY. IN NUMBER TWO, YOU SEE HOW I IMPROVED IT, STRIVING FOR A CERTAIN ELEGANCE, A SWEEPING GRANDEUR...
1. Lt. Sonny Fuzz
2. Lt. Sonny Fuzz
NOTICE, HOWEVER, IN 3 AND 4, HOW I BEGAN TO USE A HEAVIER LINE, BECOMING INCREASINGLY BOLDER....BUT, AT THE SAME TIME, IT BEGAN TO LOOK CRUDE, A LITTLE FORCED...
3. Lt Sonny Fuzz
4. Lt. Sonny Fuzz
NOW IN 5, 6 AND 7, I...UH...
HOW'S THIS FOR A FORCEFUL SIGNATURE?!
GET OUT!!
Gen. Amos Halftrack
3-22

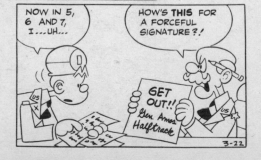

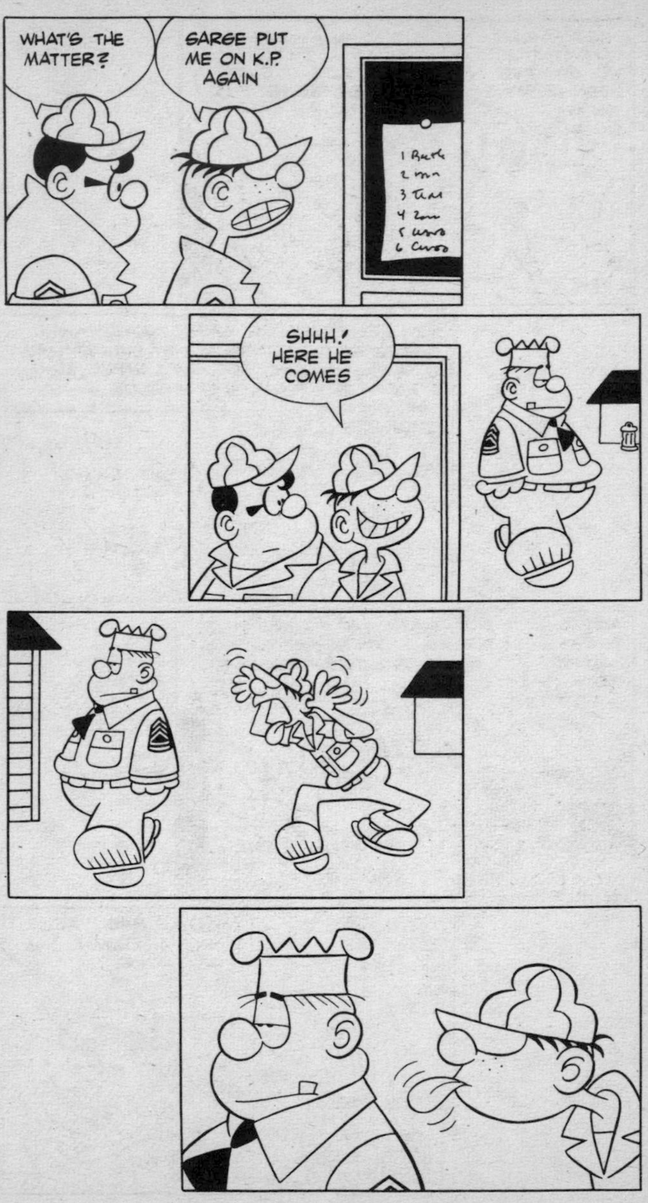
WHAT'S THE MATTER?
SARGE PUT ME ON K.P. AGAIN
SHHH! HERE HE COMES

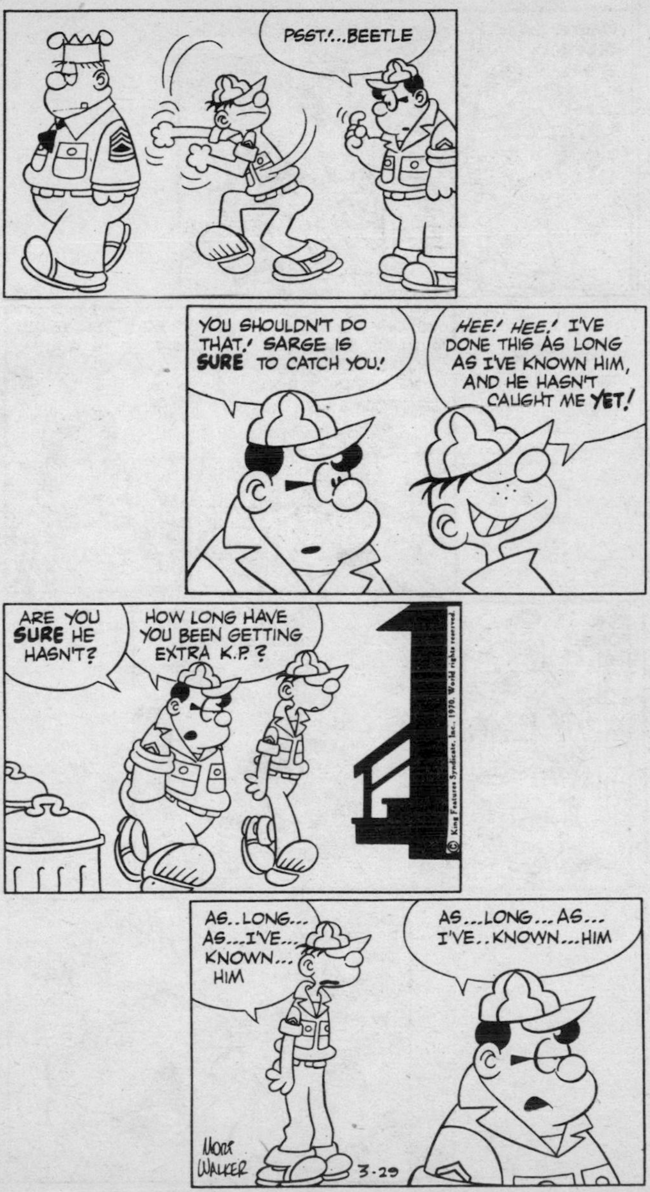
PSST.!...BEETLE
YOU SHOULDN'T DO THAT.! SARGE IS SURE TO CATCH YOU.!
HEE! HEE! I'VE DONE THIS AS LONG AS I'VE KNOWN HIM, AND HE HASN'T CAUGHT ME YET!
ARE YOU SURE HE HASN'T?
HOW LONG HAVE YOU BEEN GETTING EXTRA K.P.?
© King Features Syndicate, Inc., 1970. World rights reserved.
AS..LONG... AS...I'VE... KNOWN... HIM
AS...LONG...AS... I'VE..KNOWN...HIM
MORT WALKER
3-29

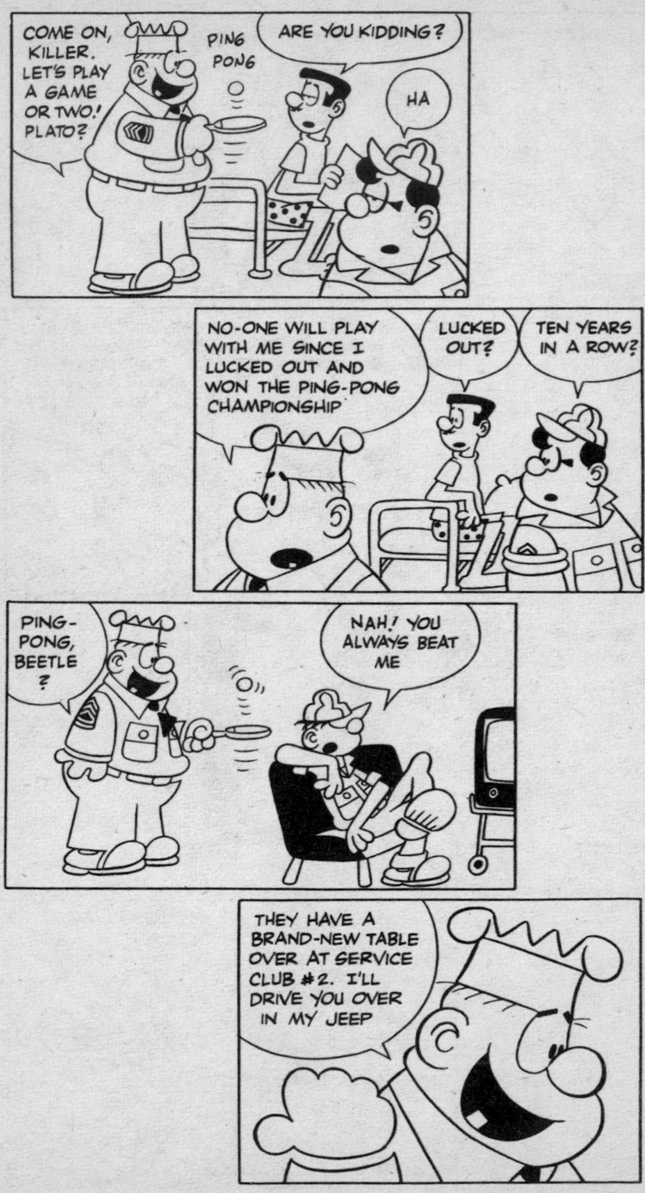
COME ON, KILLER. LET'S PLAY A GAME OR TWO! PLATO?
PING PONG
ARE YOU KIDDING?
HA
NO-ONE WILL PLAY WITH ME SINCE I LUCKED OUT AND WON THE PING-PONG CHAMPIONSHIP
LUCKED OUT?
TEN YEARS IN A ROW?
PING-PONG, BEETLE ?
NAH! YOU ALWAYS BEAT ME
THEY HAVE A BRAND-NEW TABLE OVER AT SERVICE CLUB #2. I'LL DRIVE YOU OVER IN MY JEEP

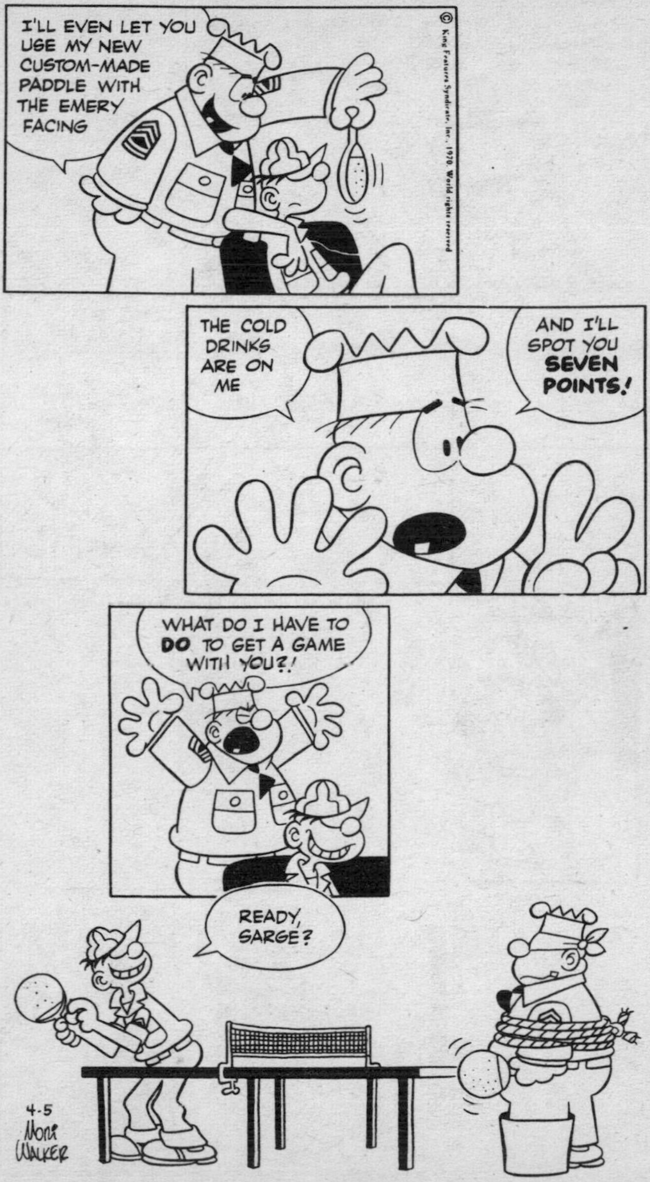
I'LL EVEN LET YOU USE MY NEW CUSTOM-MADE PADDLE WITH THE EMERY FACING
© King Features Syndicate, Inc., 1970. World rights reserved
THE COLD DRINKS ARE ON ME
AND I'LL SPOT YOU **SEVEN POINTS!**
WHAT DO I HAVE TO **DO** TO GET A GAME WITH YOU?!
READY, SARGE?
4-5
MORT WALKER

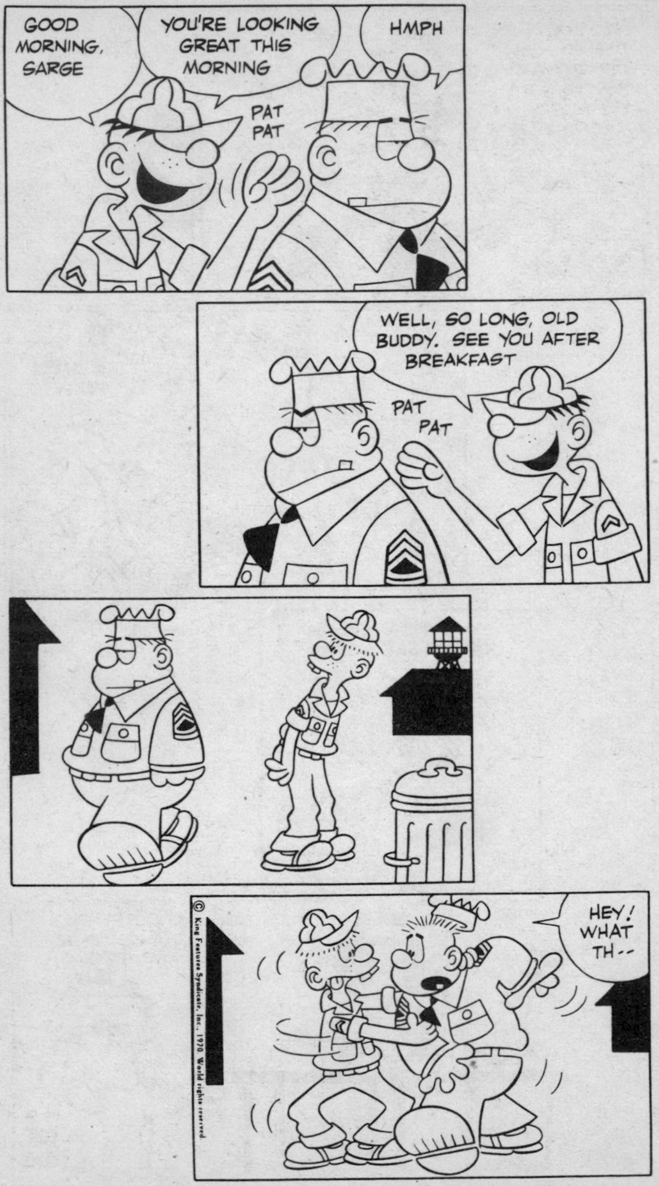

GOOD MORNING, SARGE
YOU'RE LOOKING GREAT THIS MORNING
HMPH
PAT PAT
WELL, SO LONG, OLD BUDDY. SEE YOU AFTER BREAKFAST
PAT PAT
© King Features Syndicate, Inc., 1970. World rights reserved.
HEY! WHAT TH--

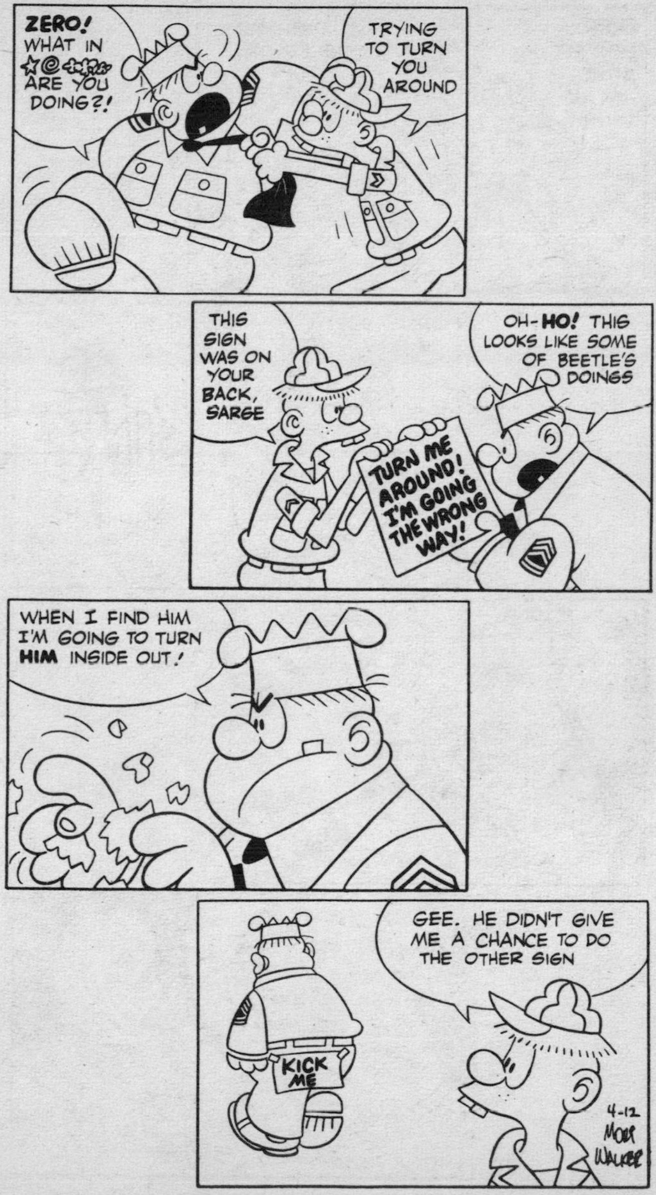
ZERO! WHAT IN ☆@✚✱✱ ARE YOU DOING?!
TRYING TO TURN YOU AROUND
THIS SIGN WAS ON YOUR BACK, SARGE
OH-HO! THIS LOOKS LIKE SOME OF BEETLE'S DOINGS
TURN ME AROUND! I'M GOING THE WRONG WAY!
WHEN I FIND HIM I'M GOING TO TURN HIM INSIDE OUT!
GEE. HE DIDN'T GIVE ME A CHANCE TO DO THE OTHER SIGN
KICK ME
4-12
MORT WALKER

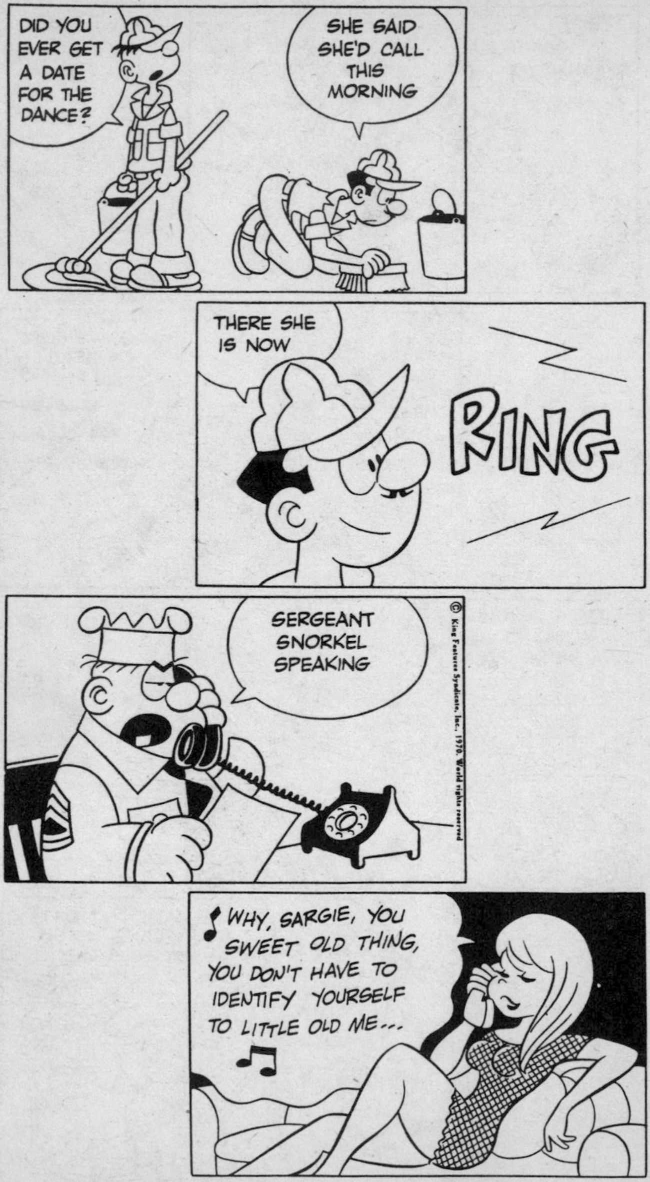
DID YOU EVER GET A DATE FOR THE DANCE?
SHE SAID SHE'D CALL THIS MORNING
THERE SHE IS NOW
RING
SERGEANT SNORKEL SPEAKING
© King Features Syndicate, Inc., 1970. World rights reserved
WHY, SARGIE, YOU SWEET OLD THING, YOU DON'T HAVE TO IDENTIFY YOURSELF TO LITTLE OLD ME...

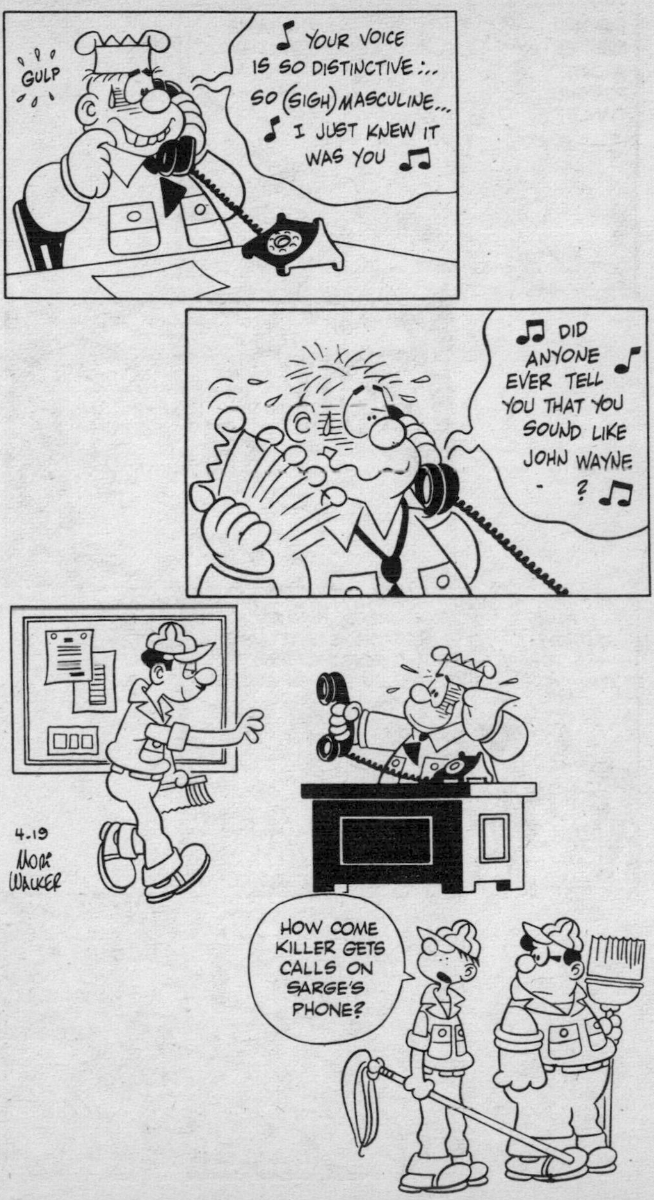
GULP
YOUR VOICE IS SO DISTINCTIVE ... SO (SIGH) MASCULINE... I JUST KNEW IT WAS YOU
DID ANYONE EVER TELL YOU THAT YOU SOUND LIKE JOHN WAYNE - ?
4-19 MORT WALKER
HOW COME KILLER GETS CALLS ON SARGE'S PHONE?

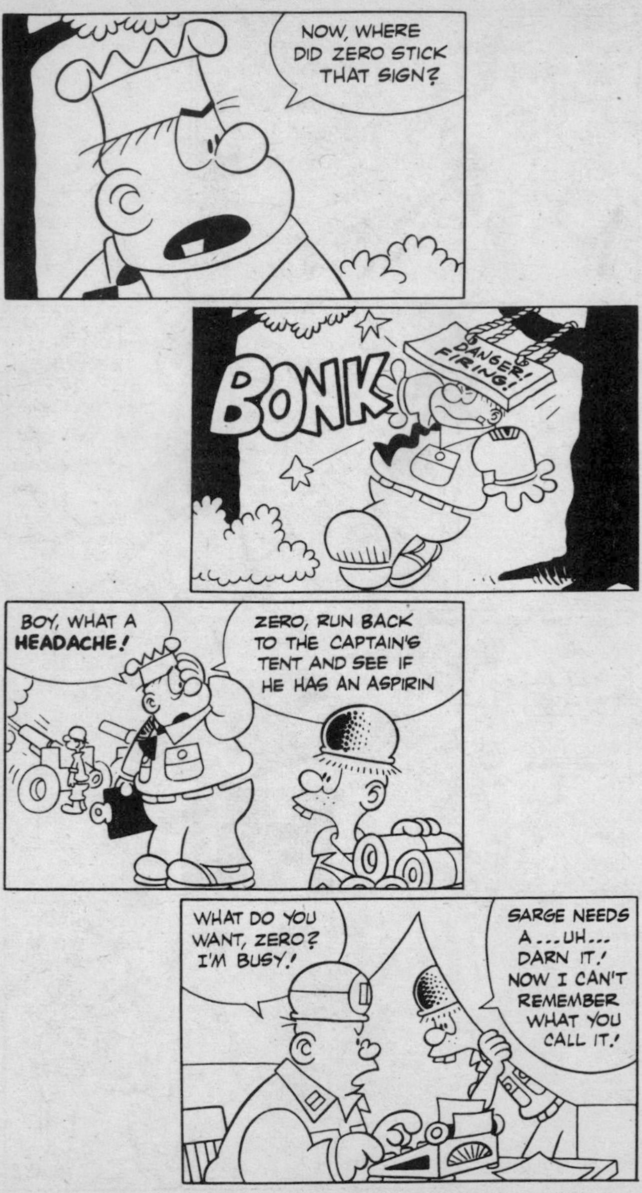
NOW, WHERE DID ZERO STICK THAT SIGN?
BONK
DANGER! FIRING!
BOY, WHAT A **HEADACHE!**
ZERO, RUN BACK TO THE CAPTAIN'S TENT AND SEE IF HE HAS AN ASPIRIN
WHAT DO YOU WANT, ZERO? I'M BUSY!
SARGE NEEDS A...UH... DARN IT! NOW I CAN'T REMEMBER WHAT YOU CALL IT!

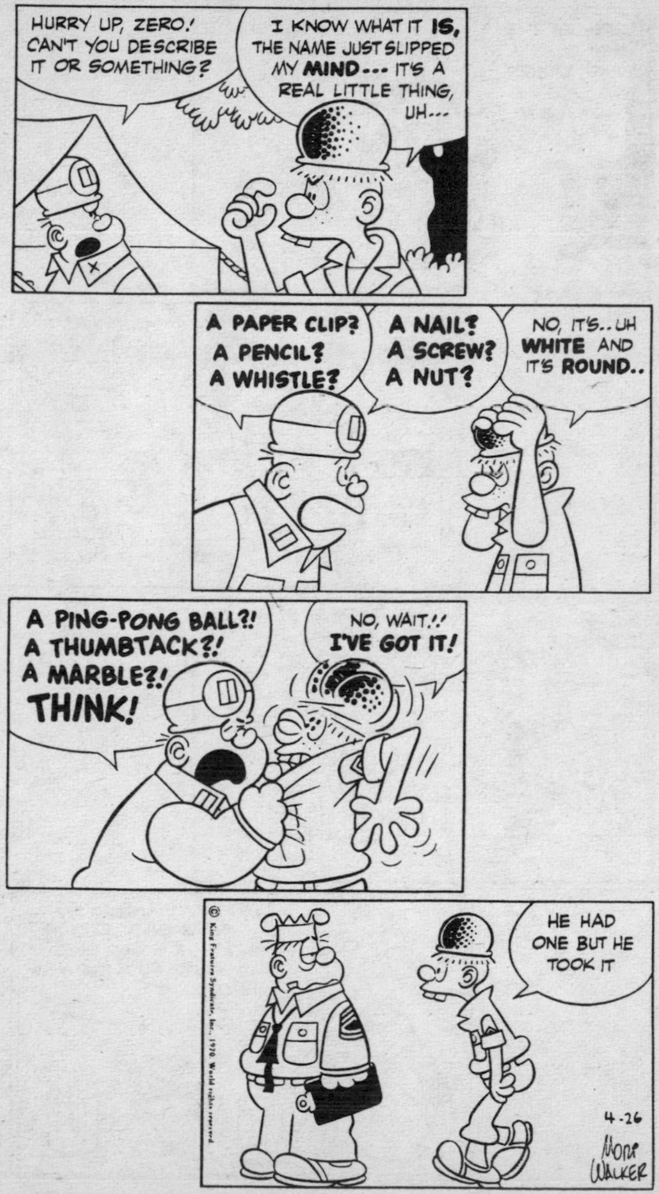
HURRY UP, ZERO! CAN'T YOU DESCRIBE IT OR SOMETHING?
I KNOW WHAT IT **IS**, THE NAME JUST SLIPPED MY **MIND**... IT'S A REAL LITTLE THING, UH...
A PAPER CLIP? A PENCIL? A WHISTLE?
A NAIL? A SCREW? A NUT?
NO, IT'S.. UH **WHITE** AND IT'S **ROUND**..
A PING-PONG BALL?! A THUMBTACK?! A MARBLE?! **THINK!**
NO, WAIT!! **I'VE GOT IT!**
© King Features Syndicate, Inc., 1970. World rights reserved.
HE HAD ONE BUT HE TOOK IT
4-26
MORT WALKER

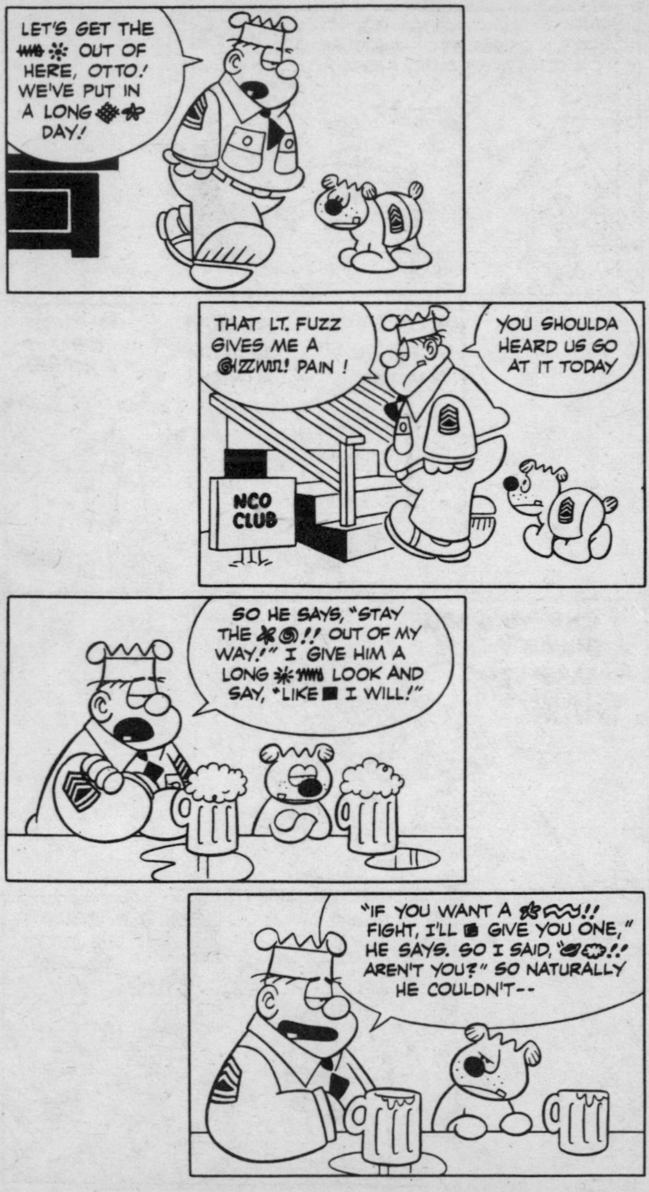
LET'S GET THE ✱✱ OUT OF HERE, OTTO! WE'VE PUT IN A LONG ✱✱ DAY!
THAT LT. FUZZ GIVES ME A ✱✱! PAIN !
YOU SHOULDA HEARD US GO AT IT TODAY
NCO CLUB
SO HE SAYS, "STAY THE ✱✱!! OUT OF MY WAY!" I GIVE HIM A LONG ✱✱ LOOK AND SAY, "LIKE ■ I WILL!"
"IF YOU WANT A ✱✱!! FIGHT, I'LL ■ GIVE YOU ONE," HE SAYS. SO I SAID, "✱✱!! AREN'T YOU?" SO NATURALLY HE COULDN'T--

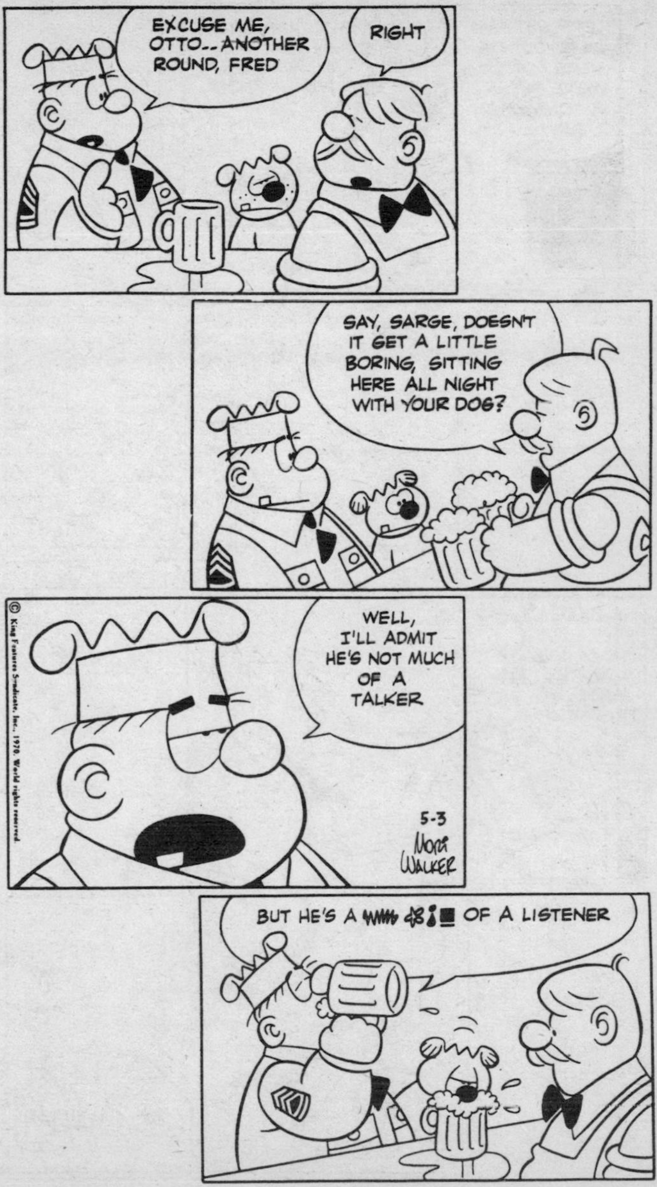
EXCUSE ME, OTTO-- ANOTHER ROUND, FRED
RIGHT
SAY, SARGE, DOESN'T IT GET A LITTLE BORING, SITTING HERE ALL NIGHT WITH YOUR DOG?
WELL, I'LL ADMIT HE'S NOT MUCH OF A TALKER
© King Features Syndicate, Inc., 1970. World rights reserved.
5-3
MORT WALKER
BUT HE'S A OF A LISTENER

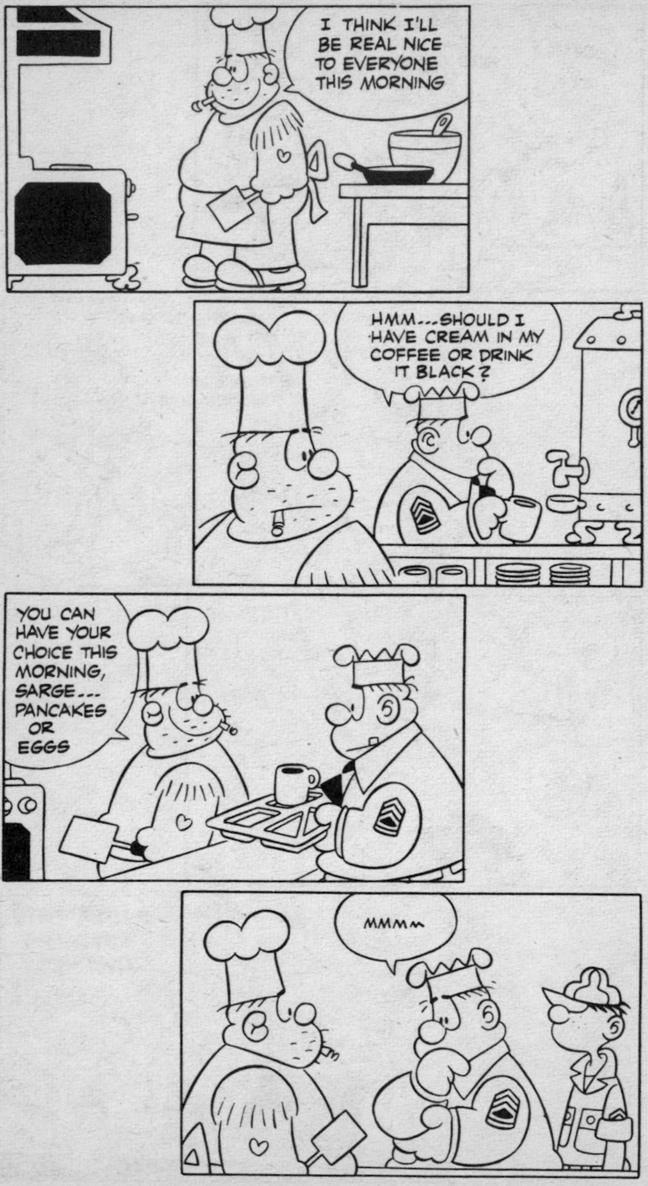
I THINK I'LL BE REAL NICE TO EVERYONE THIS MORNING
HMM...SHOULD I HAVE CREAM IN MY COFFEE OR DRINK IT BLACK?
YOU CAN HAVE YOUR CHOICE THIS MORNING, SARGE... PANCAKES OR EGGS
MMMM

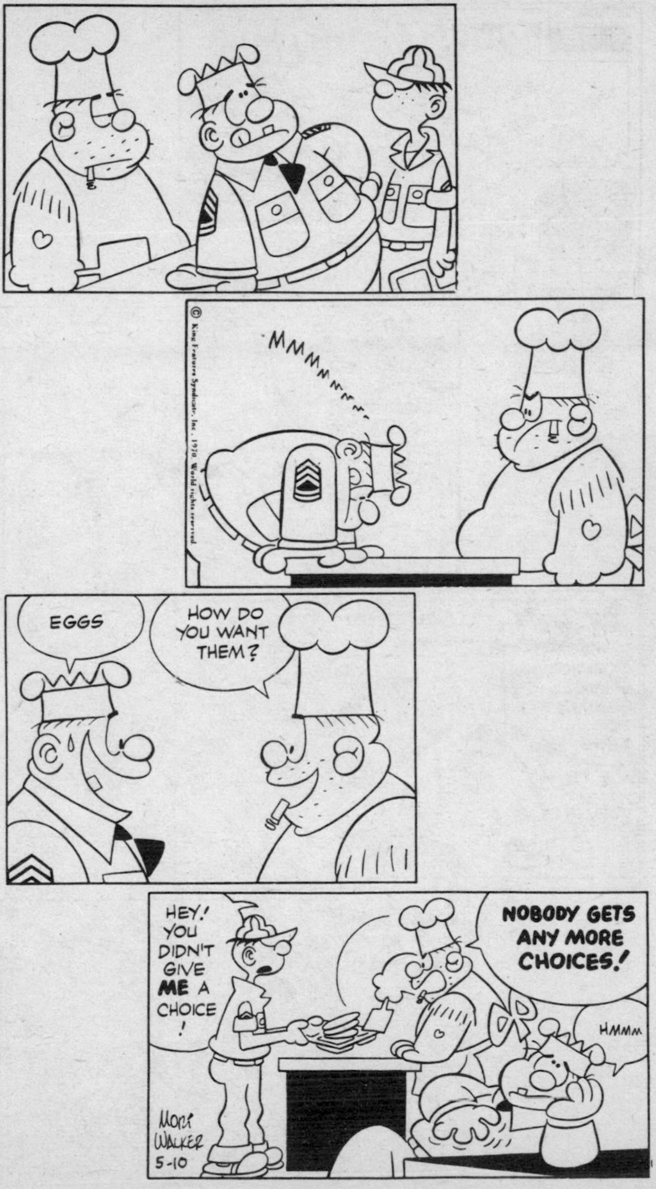
MMMMMMMM
EGGS
HOW DO YOU WANT THEM?
HEY! YOU DIDN'T GIVE **ME** A CHOICE!
NOBODY GETS ANY MORE CHOICES!
HMMM
MORT WALKER 5-10

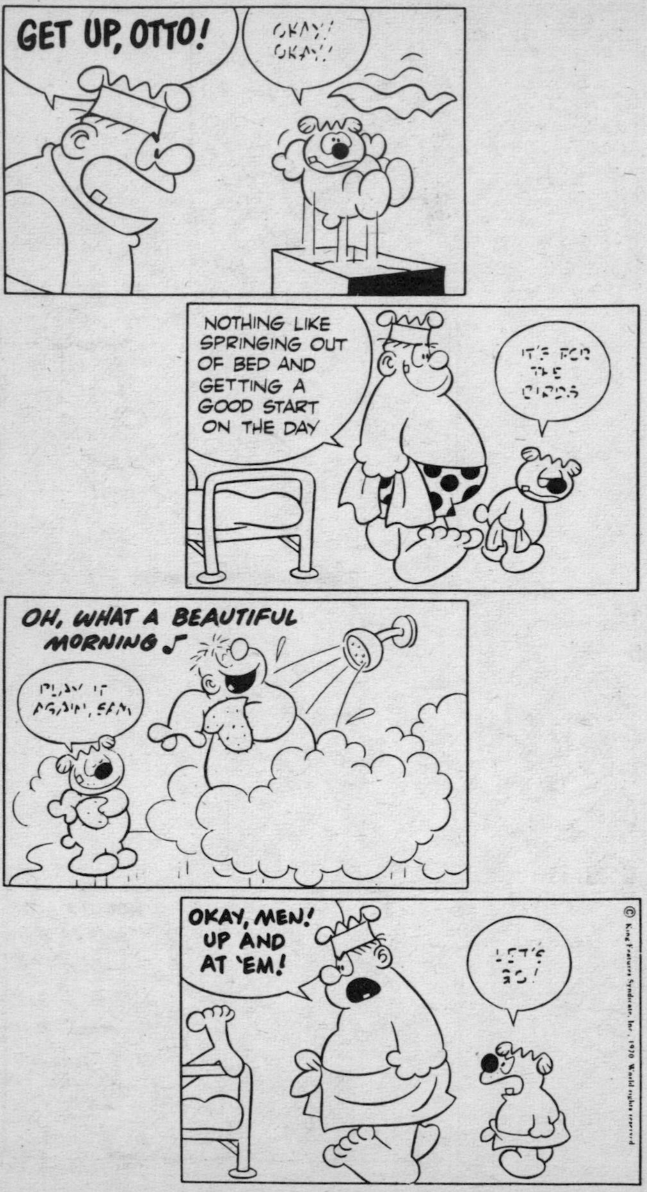
GET UP, OTTO!
OKAY! OKAY!
NOTHING LIKE SPRINGING OUT OF BED AND GETTING A GOOD START ON THE DAY
IT'S FOR THE BIRDS
OH, WHAT A BEAUTIFUL MORNING
PLAY IT AGAIN, SAM
OKAY, MEN! UP AND AT 'EM!
LET'S GO!

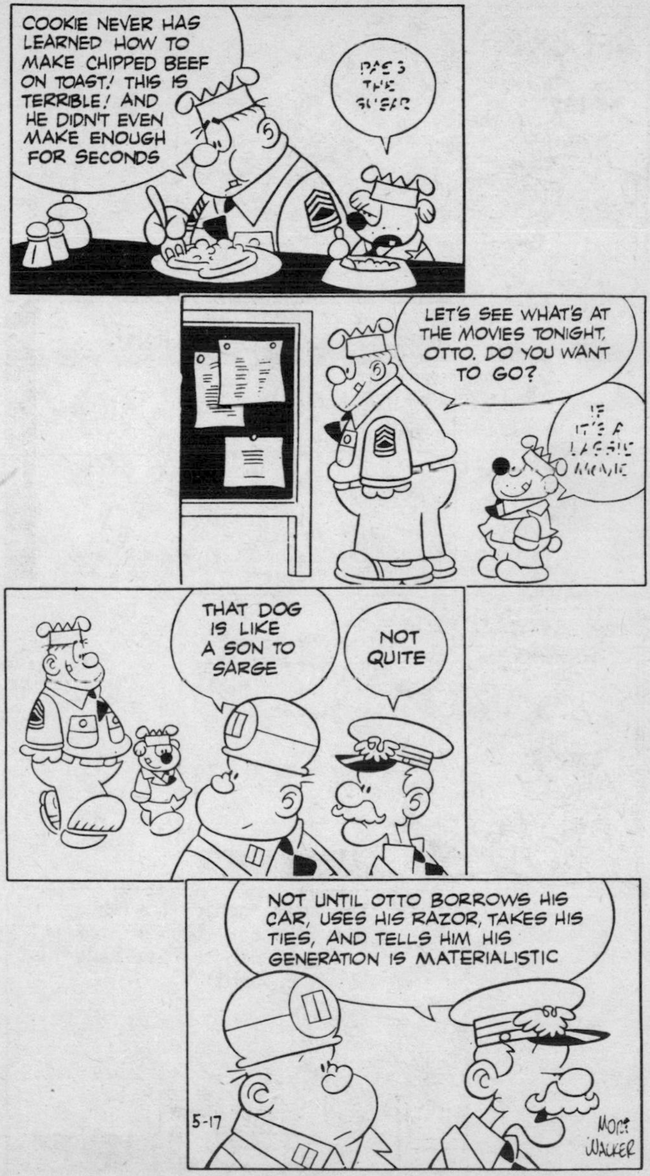
COOKIE NEVER HAS LEARNED HOW TO MAKE CHIPPED BEEF ON TOAST! THIS IS TERRIBLE! AND HE DIDN'T EVEN MAKE ENOUGH FOR SECONDS
PASS THE SUGAR
LET'S SEE WHAT'S AT THE MOVIES TONIGHT, OTTO. DO YOU WANT TO GO?
IF IT'S A LASSIE MOVIE
THAT DOG IS LIKE A SON TO SARGE
NOT QUITE
NOT UNTIL OTTO BORROWS HIS CAR, USES HIS RAZOR, TAKES HIS TIES, AND TELLS HIM HIS GENERATION IS MATERIALISTIC
5-17
MORT WALKER

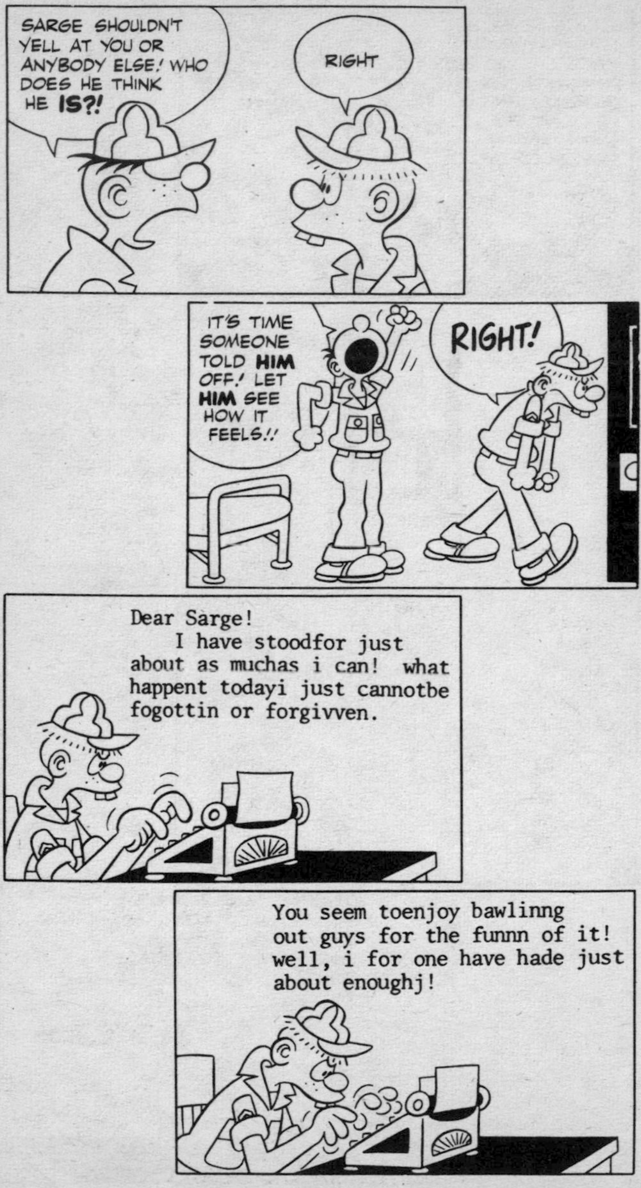
SARGE SHOULDN'T YELL AT YOU OR ANYBODY ELSE! WHO DOES HE THINK HE IS?!
RIGHT
IT'S TIME SOMEONE TOLD HIM OFF! LET HIM SEE HOW IT FEELS!!
RIGHT!
Dear Sarge!
I have stoodfor just about as muchas i can! what happent todayi just cannotbe fogottin or forgivven.
You seem toenjoy bawlinng out guys for the funnn of it! well, i for one have hade just about enoughj!

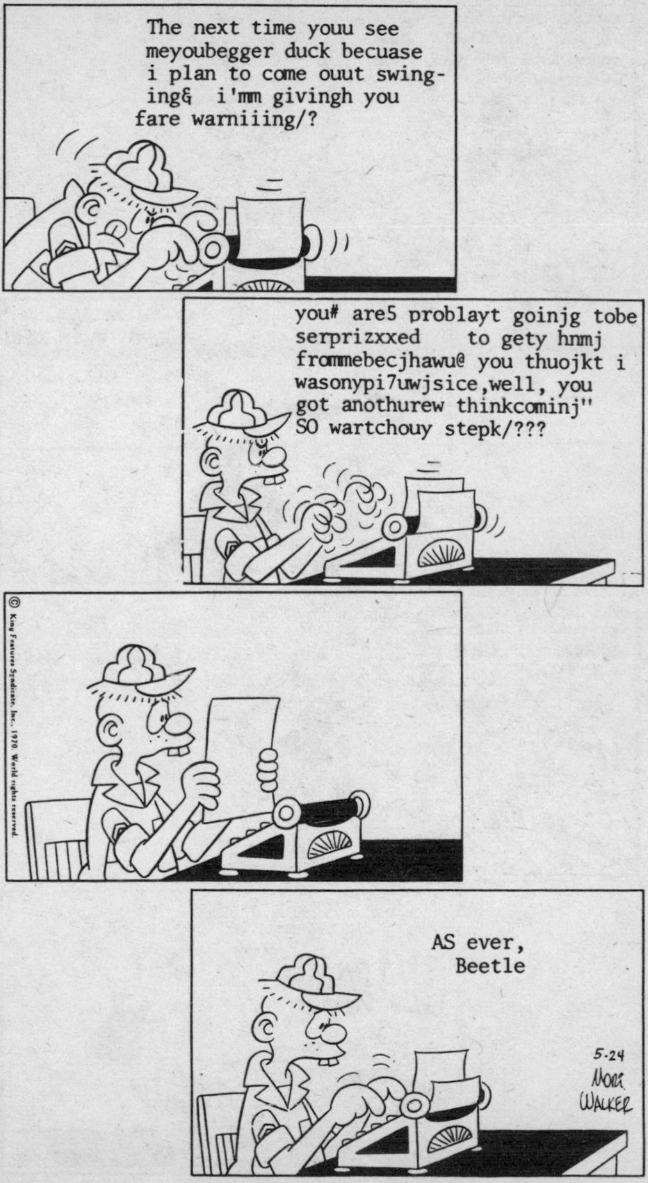
The next time youu see
meyoubegger duck becuase
i plan to come ouut swing-
ing& i'mm givingh you
fare warniiing/?
you# are5 problayt goinjg tobe
serprizxxed to gety hnmj
frommebecjhawu@ you thuojkt i
wasonypi7uwjsice,well, you
got anothurew thinkcominj"
SO wartchouy stepk/???
© King Features Syndicate, Inc., 1970. World rights reserved.
AS ever,
Beetle
5-24
MORT WALKER

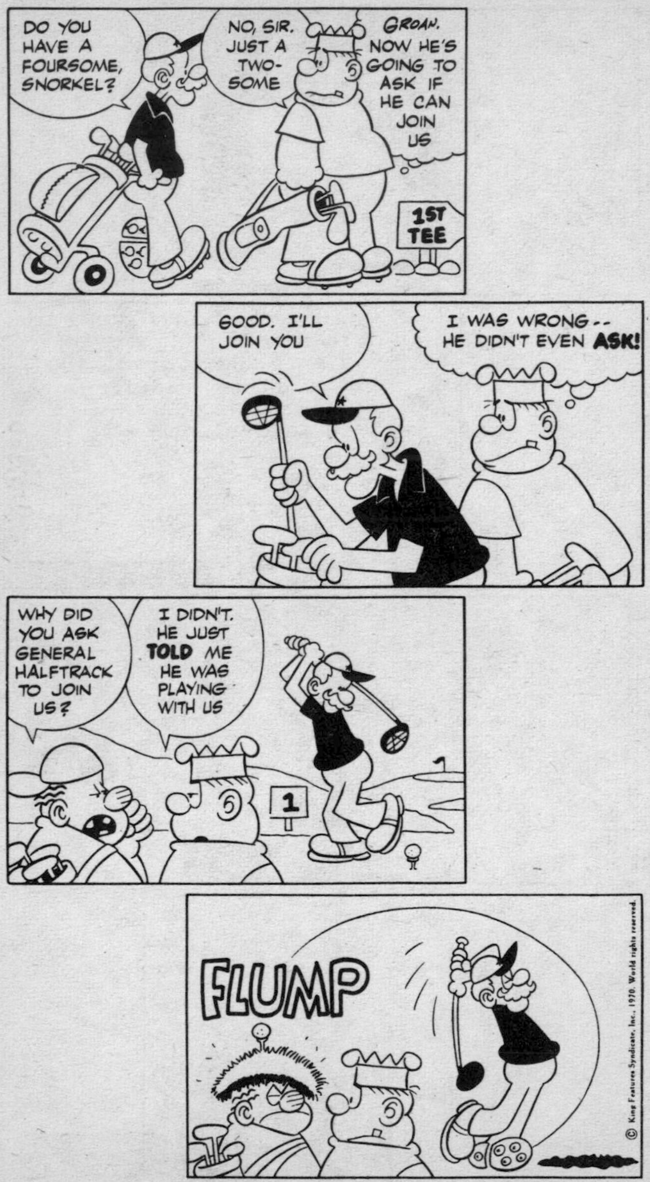
DO YOU HAVE A FOURSOME, SNORKEL?
NO, SIR. JUST A TWO-SOME
GROAN. NOW HE'S GOING TO ASK IF HE CAN JOIN US
1ST TEE
GOOD. I'LL JOIN YOU
I WAS WRONG-- HE DIDN'T EVEN ASK!
WHY DID YOU ASK GENERAL HALFTRACK TO JOIN US?
I DIDN'T. HE JUST TOLD ME HE WAS PLAYING WITH US
1
FLUMP

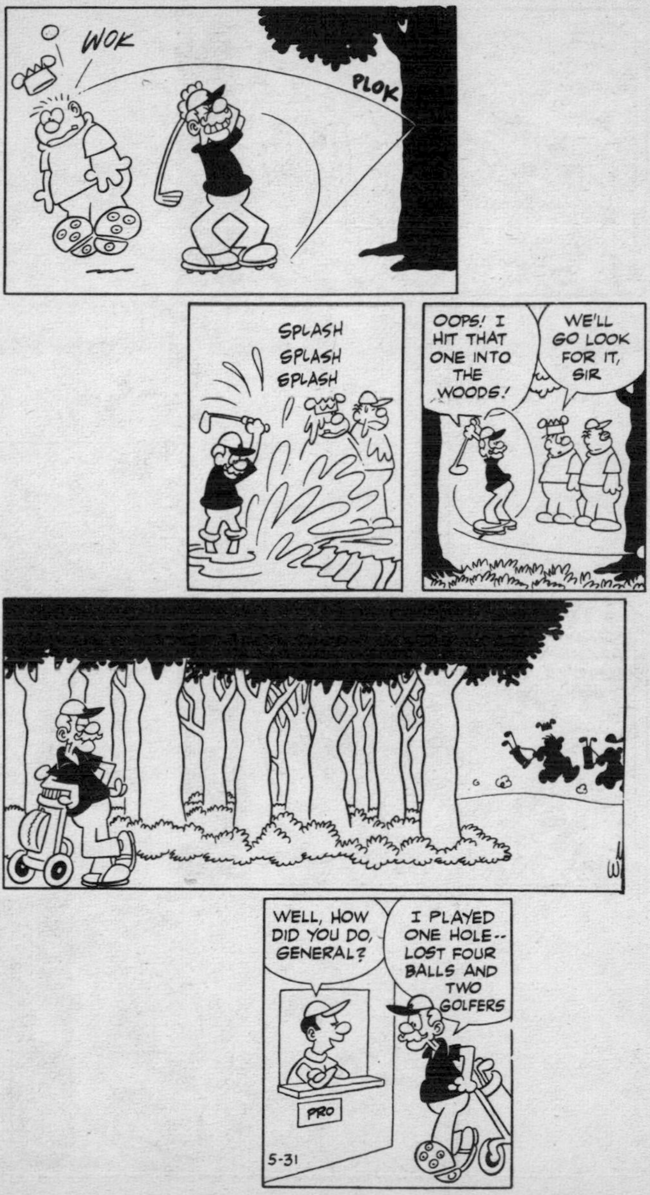
WOK
PLOK
SPLASH
SPLASH
SPLASH
OOPS! I HIT THAT ONE INTO THE WOODS!
WE'LL GO LOOK FOR IT, SIR
WELL, HOW DID YOU DO, GENERAL?
I PLAYED ONE HOLE-- LOST FOUR BALLS AND TWO GOLFERS
PRO
5-31

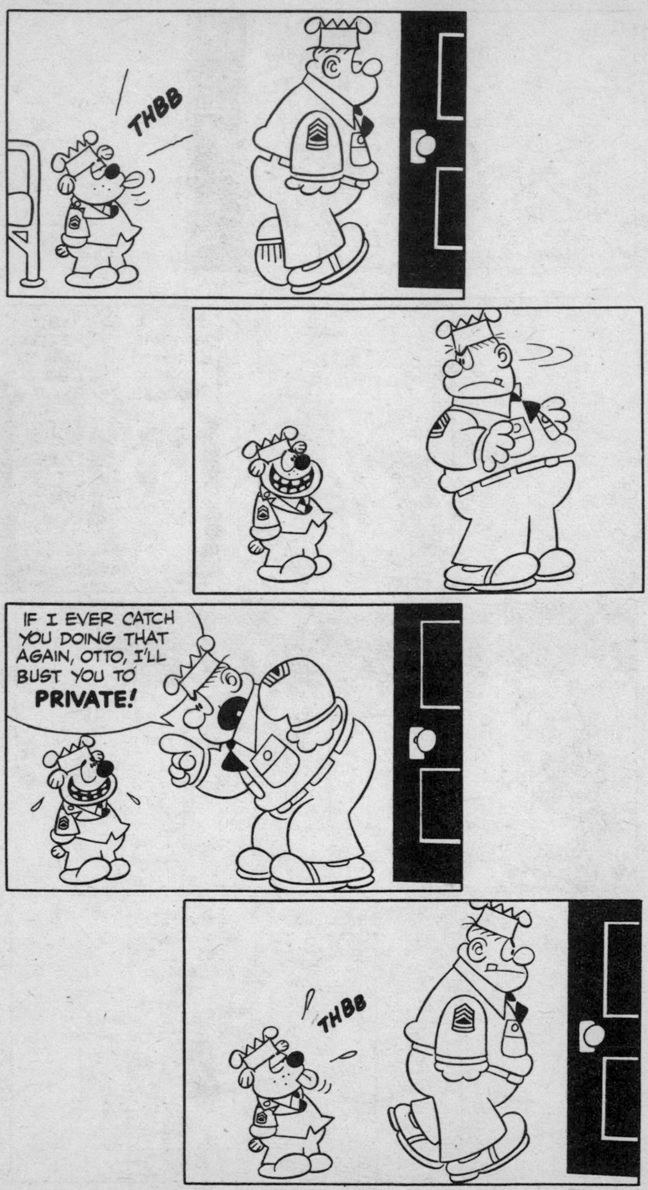
THBB
IF I EVER CATCH YOU DOING THAT AGAIN, OTTO, I'LL BUST YOU TO **PRIVATE!**
THBB

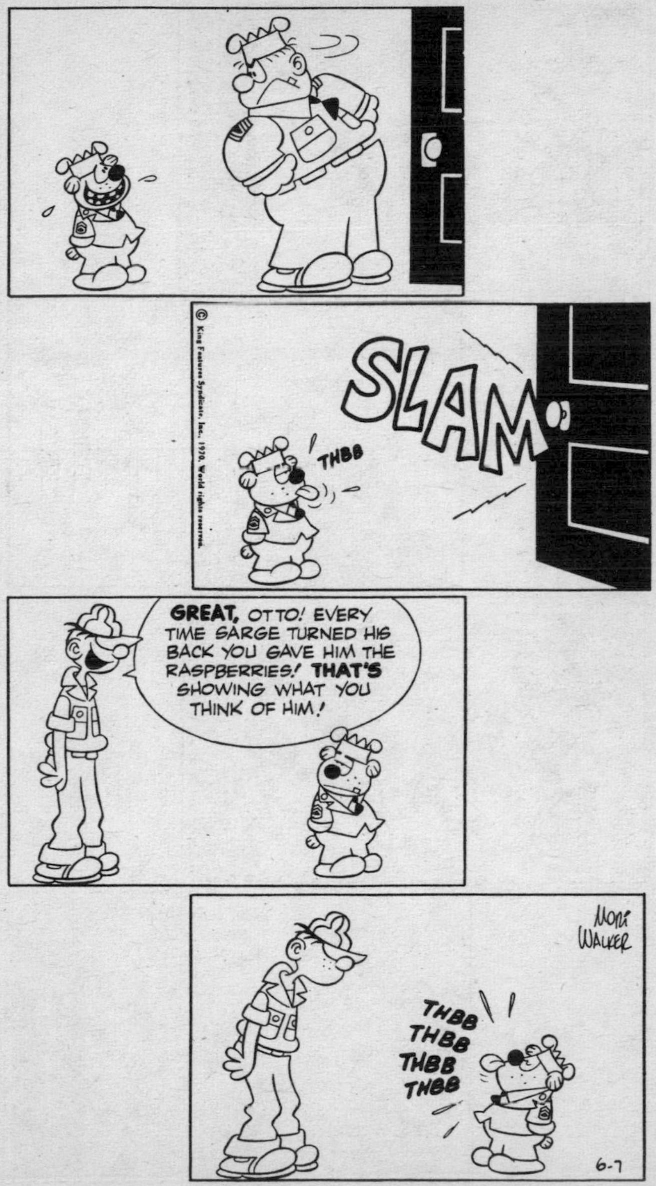
© King Features Syndicate, Inc., 1970. World rights reserved.
SLAM
THBB
GREAT, OTTO! EVERY TIME SARGE TURNED HIS BACK YOU GAVE HIM THE RASPBERRIES! THAT'S SHOWING WHAT YOU THINK OF HIM!
MORT WALKER
THBB THBB THBB THBB
6-7

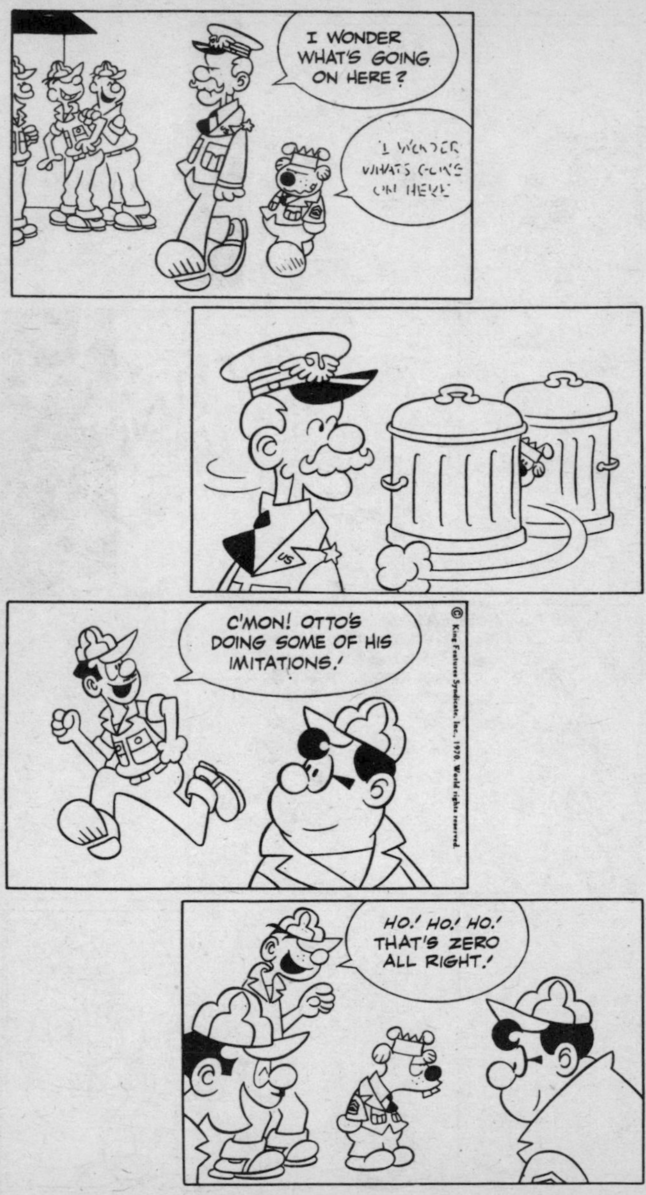
I WONDER WHAT'S GOING ON HERE?
C'MON! OTTO'S DOING SOME OF HIS IMITATIONS!
© King Features Syndicate, Inc., 1970. World rights reserved.
HO! HO! HO! THAT'S ZERO ALL RIGHT!

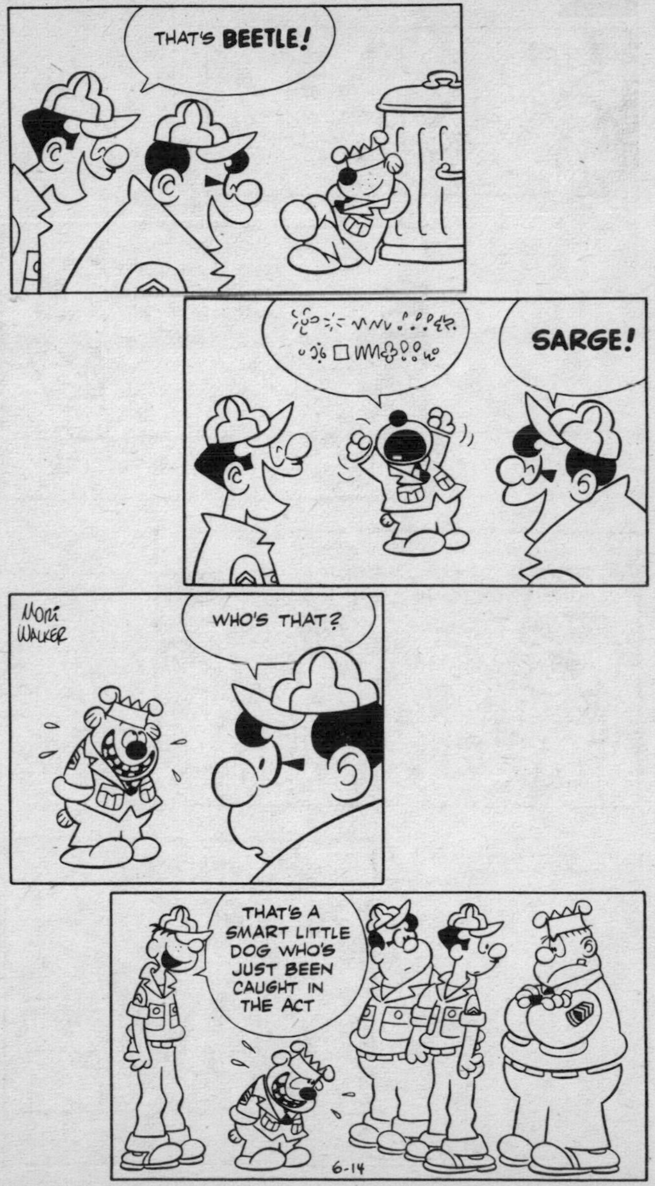
THAT'S BEETLE!
SARGE!
MORT WALKER
WHO'S THAT?
THAT'S A SMART LITTLE DOG WHO'S JUST BEEN CAUGHT IN THE ACT
6-14

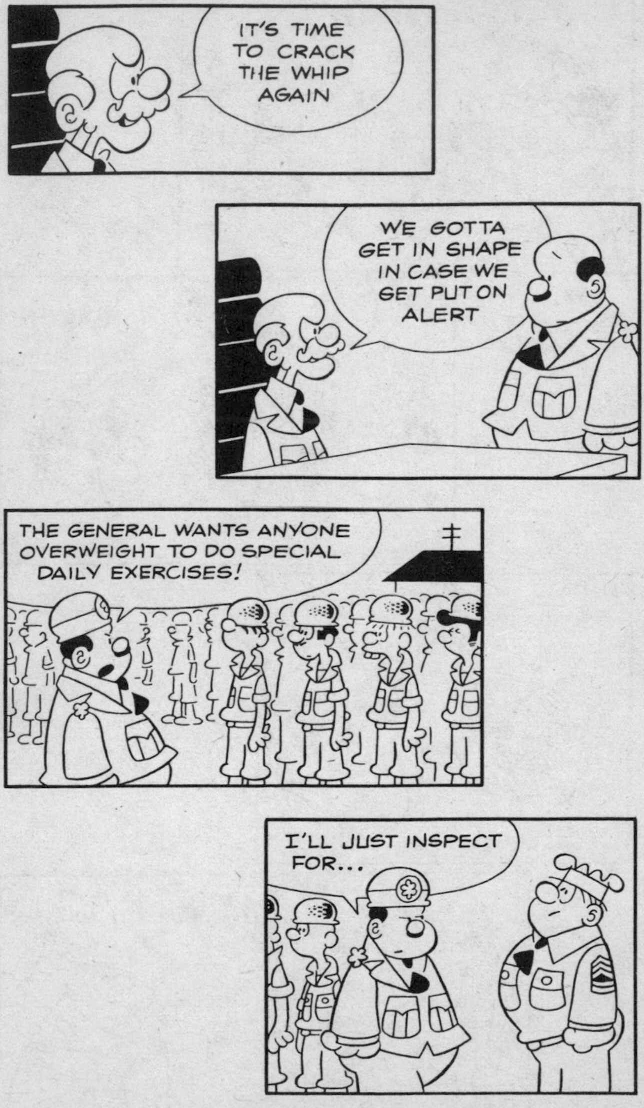
IT'S TIME TO CRACK THE WHIP AGAIN
WE GOTTA GET IN SHAPE IN CASE WE GET PUT ON ALERT
THE GENERAL WANTS ANYONE OVERWEIGHT TO DO SPECIAL DAILY EXERCISES!
I'LL JUST INSPECT FOR...

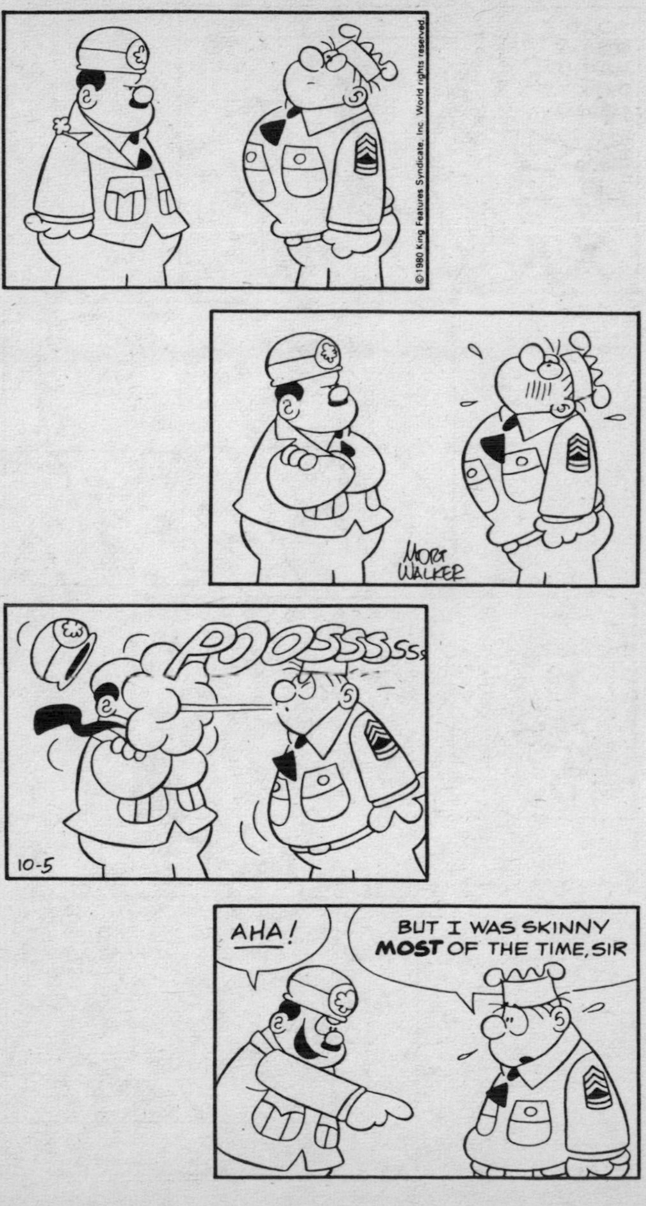
© 1980 King Features Syndicate, Inc. World rights reserved.
MORT WALKER
POOSSSSSss
10-5
AHA!
BUT I WAS SKINNY MOST OF THE TIME, SIR

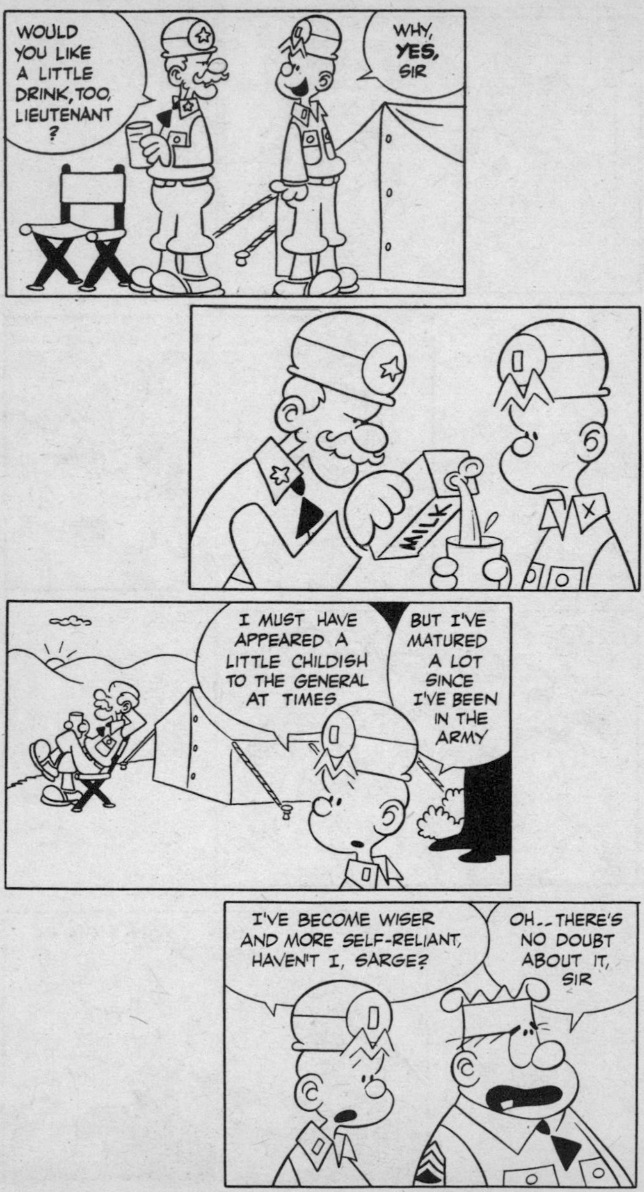
WOULD YOU LIKE A LITTLE DRINK, TOO, LIEUTENANT?
WHY, **YES,** SIR
MILK
I MUST HAVE APPEARED A LITTLE CHILDISH TO THE GENERAL AT TIMES
BUT I'VE MATURED A LOT SINCE I'VE BEEN IN THE ARMY
I'VE BECOME WISER AND MORE SELF-RELIANT, HAVEN'T I, SARGE?
OH.. THERE'S NO DOUBT ABOUT IT, SIR

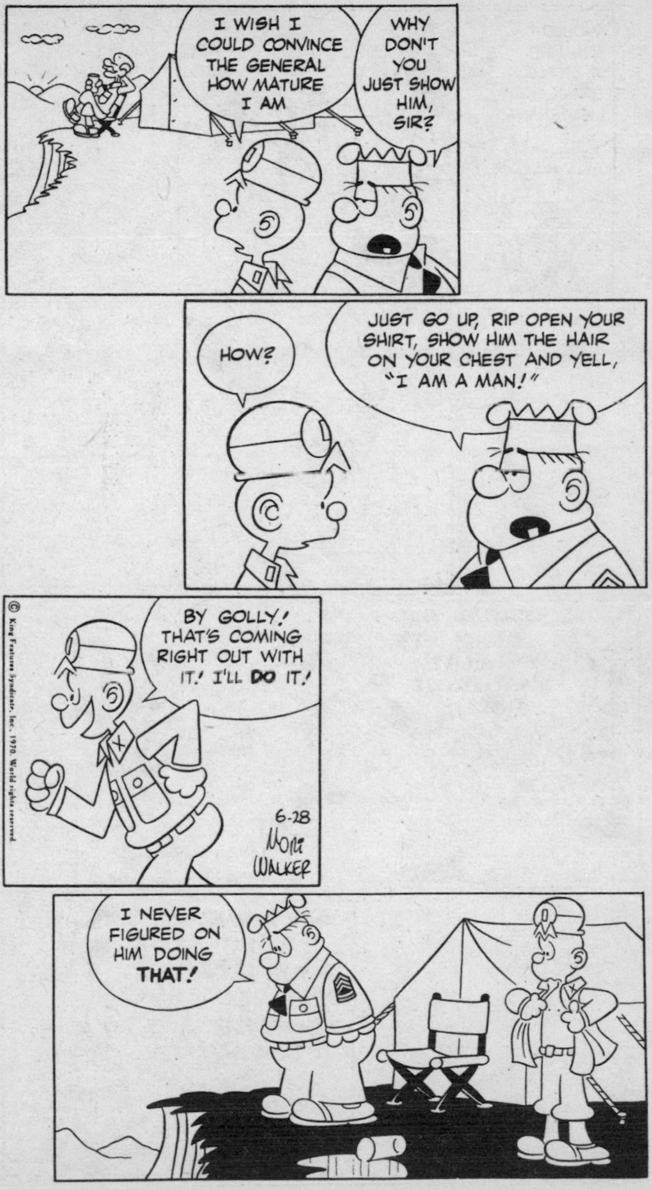
I WISH I COULD CONVINCE THE GENERAL HOW MATURE I AM
WHY DON'T YOU JUST SHOW HIM, SIR?
HOW?
JUST GO UP, RIP OPEN YOUR SHIRT, SHOW HIM THE HAIR ON YOUR CHEST AND YELL, "I AM A MAN!"
© King Features Syndicate, Inc., 1970. World rights reserved.
BY GOLLY! THAT'S COMING RIGHT OUT WITH IT! I'LL **DO** IT!
6-28
MORT WALKER
I NEVER FIGURED ON HIM DOING **THAT!**

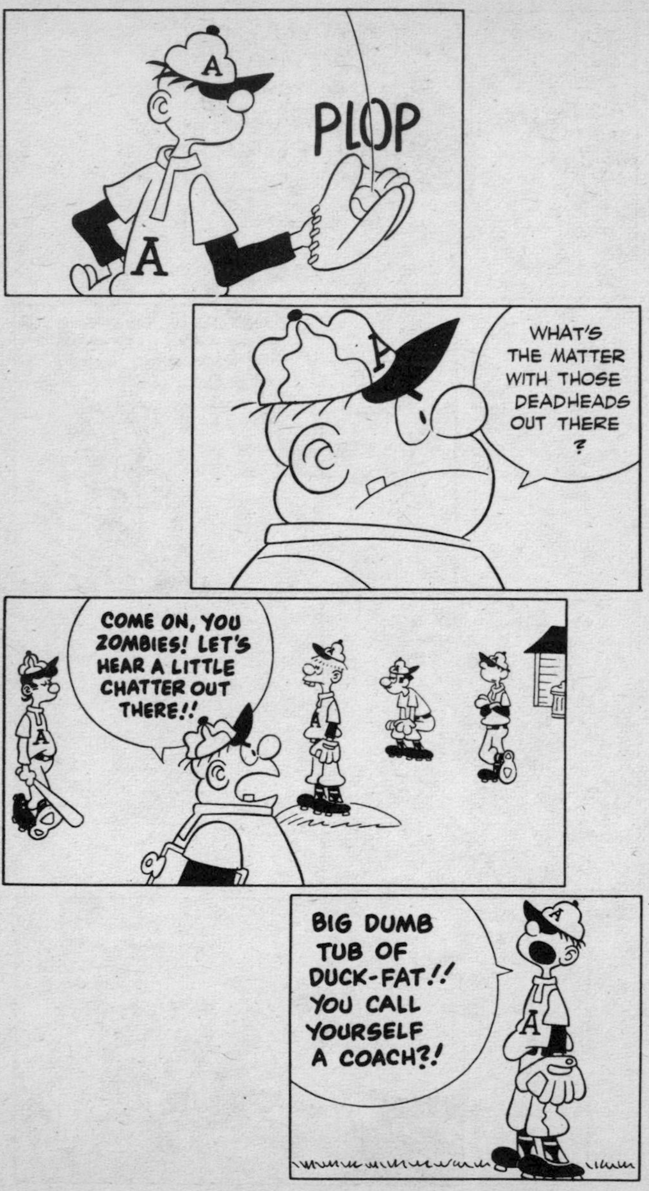
PLOP
WHAT'S THE MATTER WITH THOSE DEADHEADS OUT THERE ?
COME ON, YOU ZOMBIES! LET'S HEAR A LITTLE CHATTER OUT THERE!!
BIG DUMB TUB OF DUCK-FAT!! YOU CALL YOURSELF A COACH?!

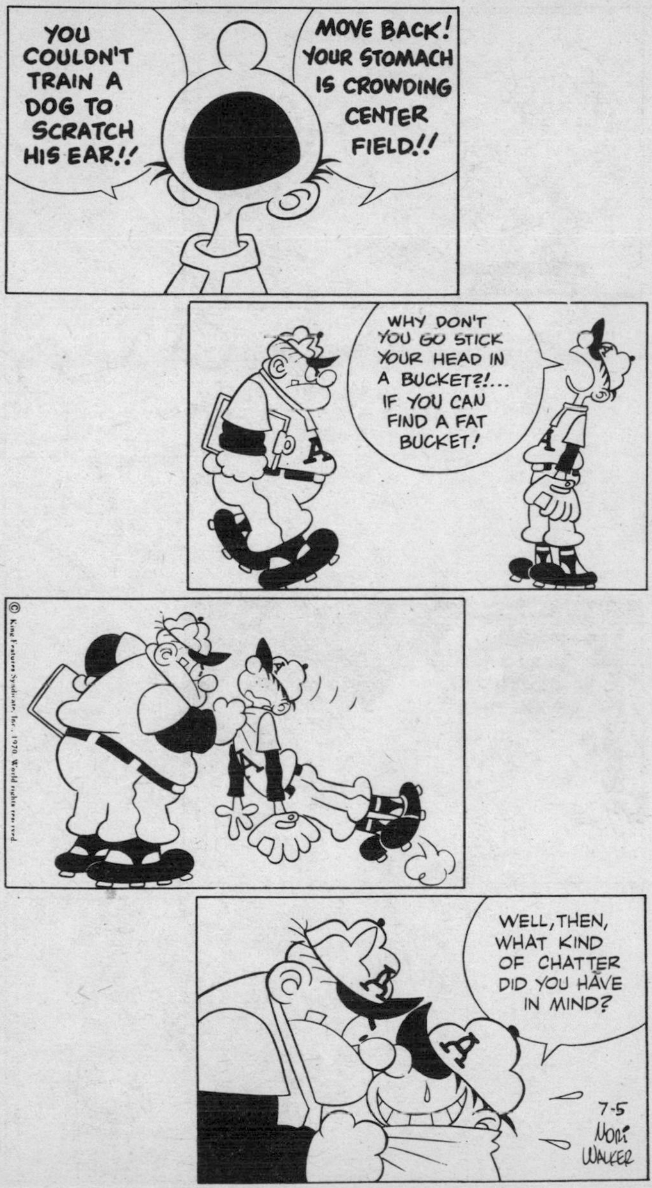
YOU COULDN'T TRAIN A DOG TO SCRATCH HIS EAR!!
MOVE BACK! YOUR STOMACH IS CROWDING CENTER FIELD!!
WHY DON'T YOU GO STICK YOUR HEAD IN A BUCKET?!... IF YOU CAN FIND A FAT BUCKET!
© King Features Syndicate, Inc., 1970 World rights reserved.
WELL, THEN, WHAT KIND OF CHATTER DID YOU HAVE IN MIND?
7-5
MORT WALKER

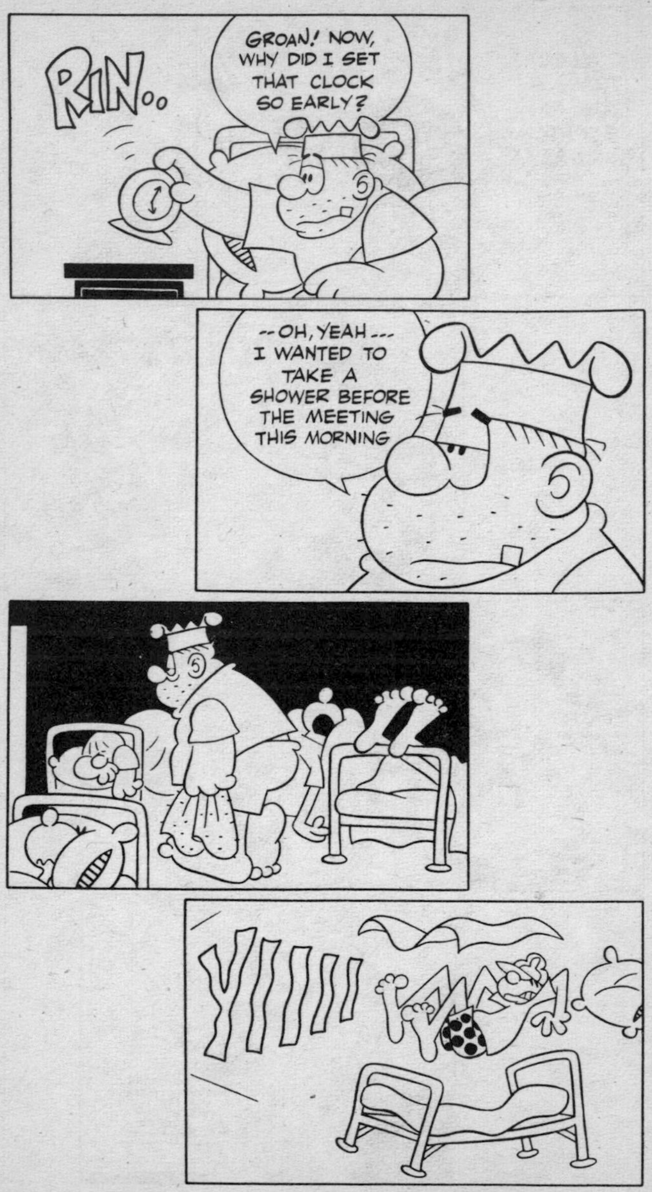
RIN..
GROAN! NOW, WHY DID I SET THAT CLOCK SO EARLY?
--OH, YEAH--- I WANTED TO TAKE A SHOWER BEFORE THE MEETING THIS MORNING
YIIIII

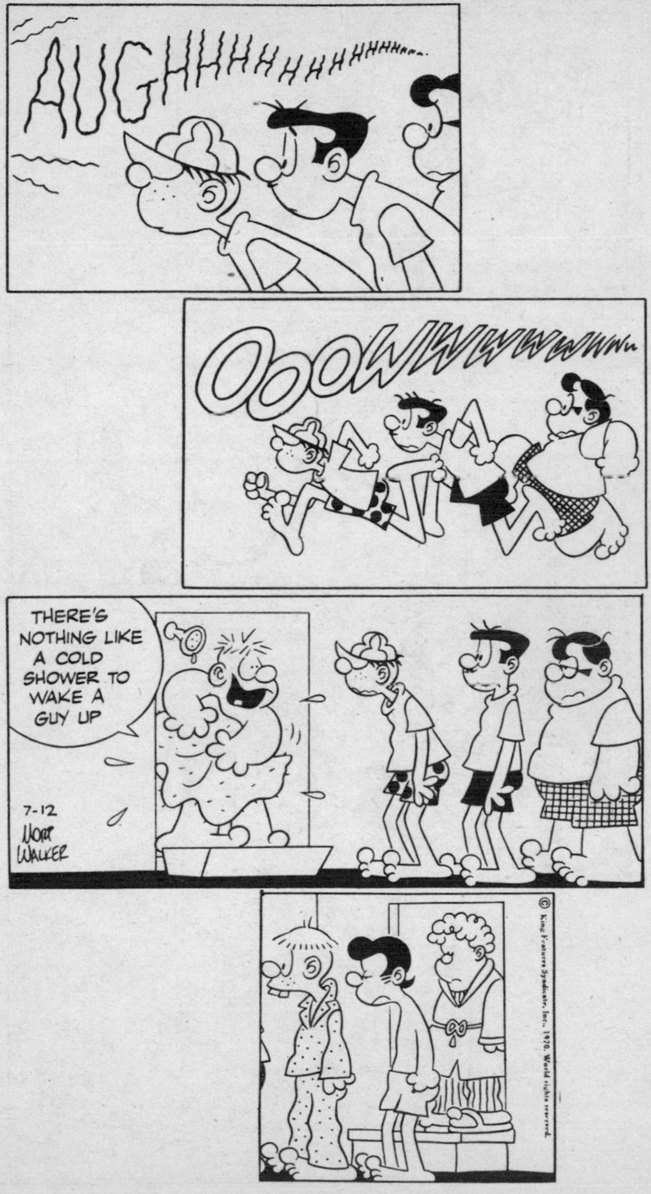
AUGHHHHHHHHHHH...
OOOWWWWWWWW...
THERE'S NOTHING LIKE A COLD SHOWER TO WAKE A GUY UP
7-12
MORT WALKER
© King Features Syndicate, Inc., 1970. World rights reserved.

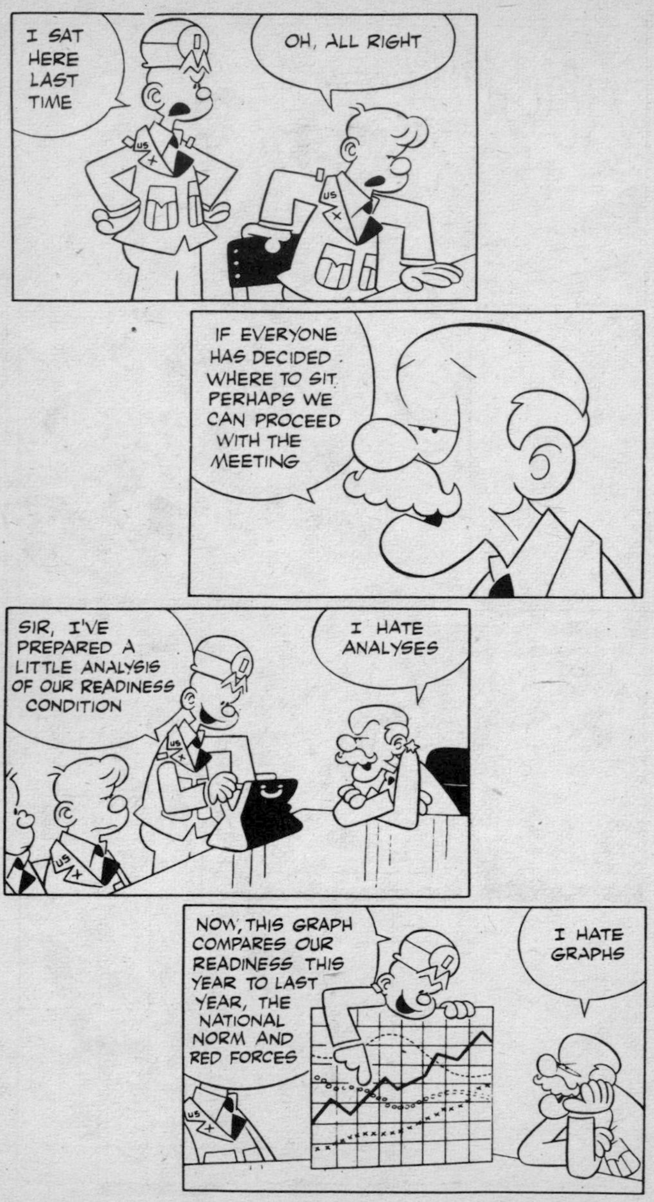
I SAT HERE LAST TIME
OH, ALL RIGHT
IF EVERYONE HAS DECIDED WHERE TO SIT PERHAPS WE CAN PROCEED WITH THE MEETING
SIR, I'VE PREPARED A LITTLE ANALYSIS OF OUR READINESS CONDITION
I HATE ANALYSES
NOW, THIS GRAPH COMPARES OUR READINESS THIS YEAR TO LAST YEAR, THE NATIONAL NORM AND RED FORCES
I HATE GRAPHS

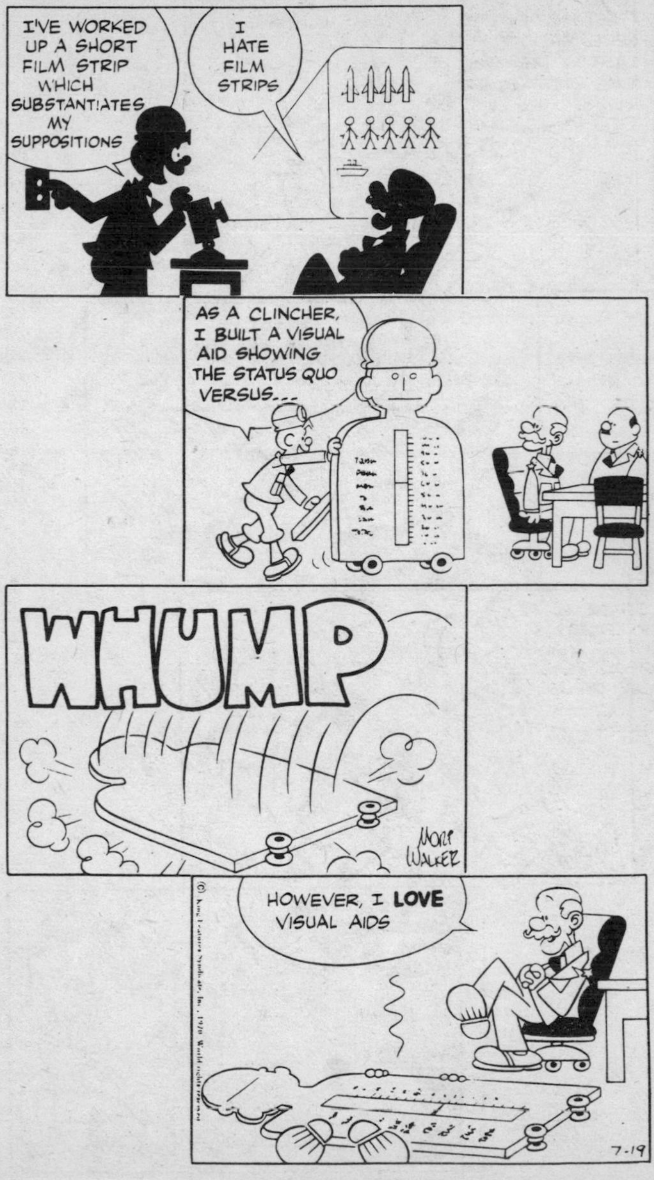
I'VE WORKED UP A SHORT FILM STRIP WHICH SUBSTANTIATES MY SUPPOSITIONS
I HATE FILM STRIPS
AS A CLINCHER, I BUILT A VISUAL AID SHOWING THE STATUS QUO VERSUS...
WHUMP
MORT WALKER
© King Features Syndicate, Inc., 1970 World rights reserved
HOWEVER, I **LOVE** VISUAL AIDS
7-19

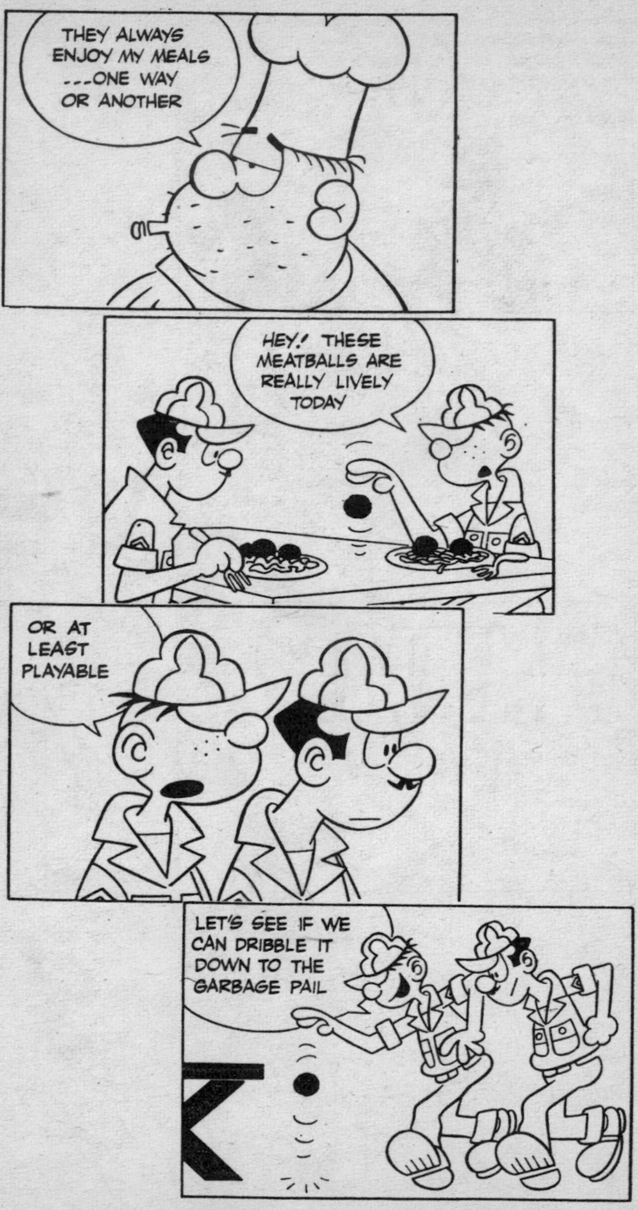
THEY ALWAYS ENJOY MY MEALS ---ONE WAY OR ANOTHER
HEY! THESE MEATBALLS ARE REALLY LIVELY TODAY
OR AT LEAST PLAYABLE
LET'S SEE IF WE CAN DRIBBLE IT DOWN TO THE GARBAGE PAIL

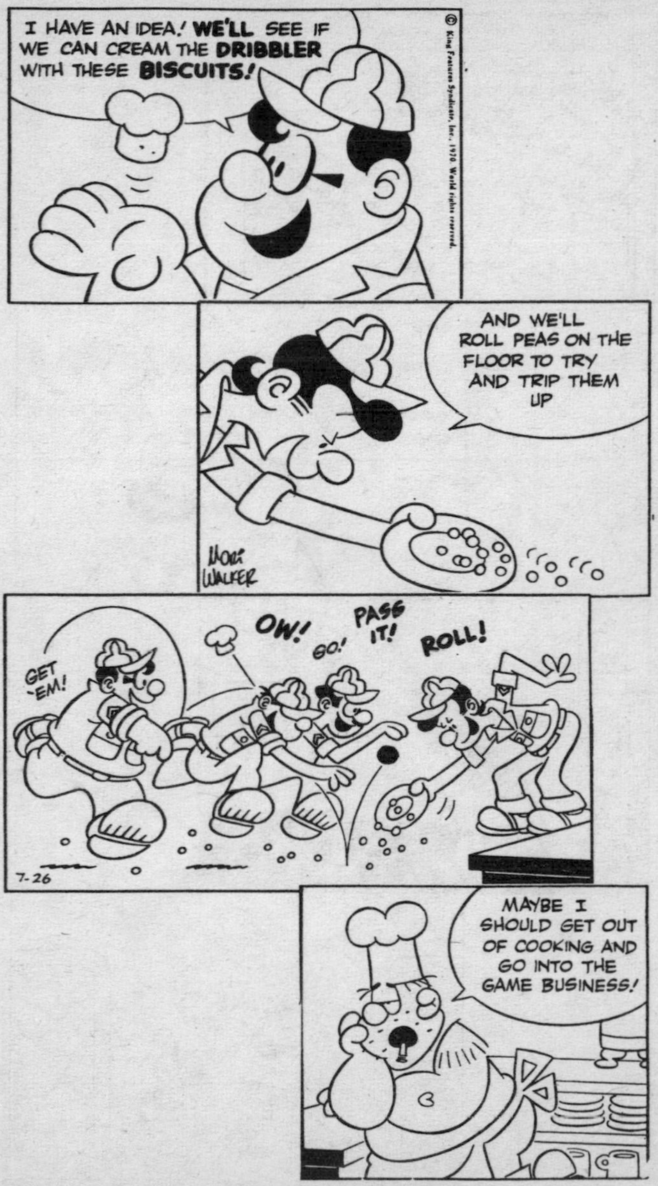
I HAVE AN IDEA! WE'LL SEE IF WE CAN CREAM THE DRIBBLER WITH THESE BISCUITS!
© King Features Syndicate, Inc., 1970. World rights reserved.
AND WE'LL ROLL PEAS ON THE FLOOR TO TRY AND TRIP THEM UP
MORT WALKER
GET -EM!
OW!
GO!
PASS IT!
ROLL!
7-26
MAYBE I SHOULD GET OUT OF COOKING AND GO INTO THE GAME BUSINESS!

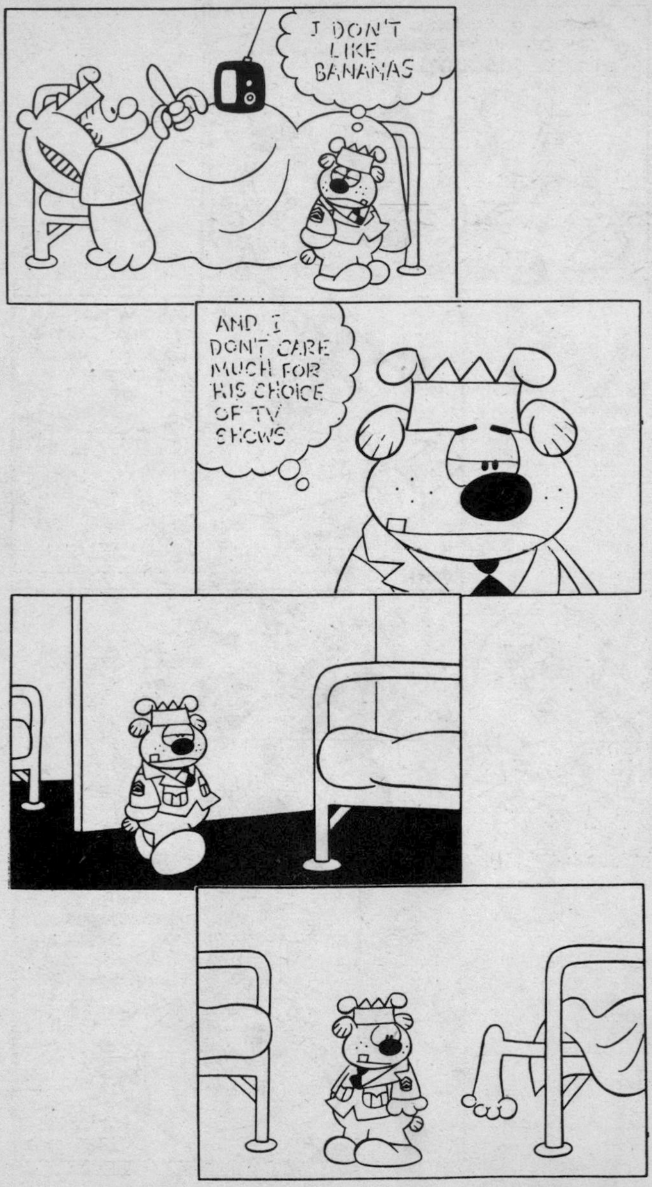
I DON'T LIKE BANANAS
AND I DON'T CARE MUCH FOR HIS CHOICE OF TV SHOWS

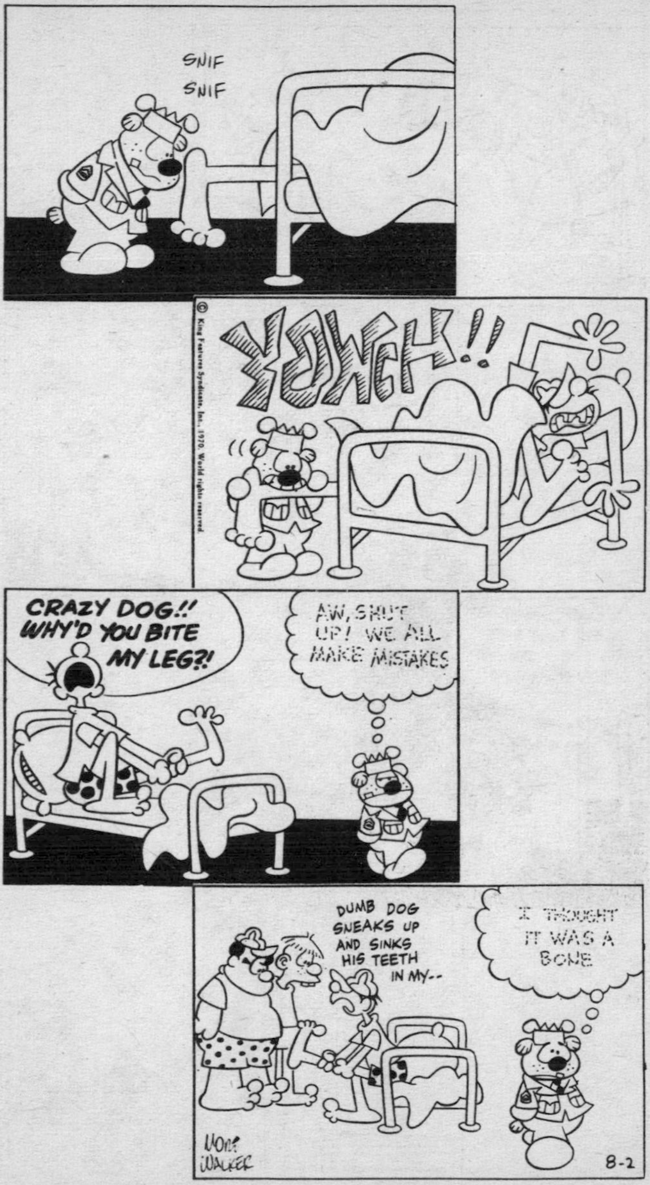
SNIF
SNIF
YOWCH!!
CRAZY DOG!! WHY'D YOU BITE MY LEG?!
AW, SHUT UP! WE ALL MAKE MISTAKES
DUMB DOG SNEAKS UP AND SINKS HIS TEETH IN MY--
I THOUGHT IT WAS A BONE
MORT WALKER
8-2

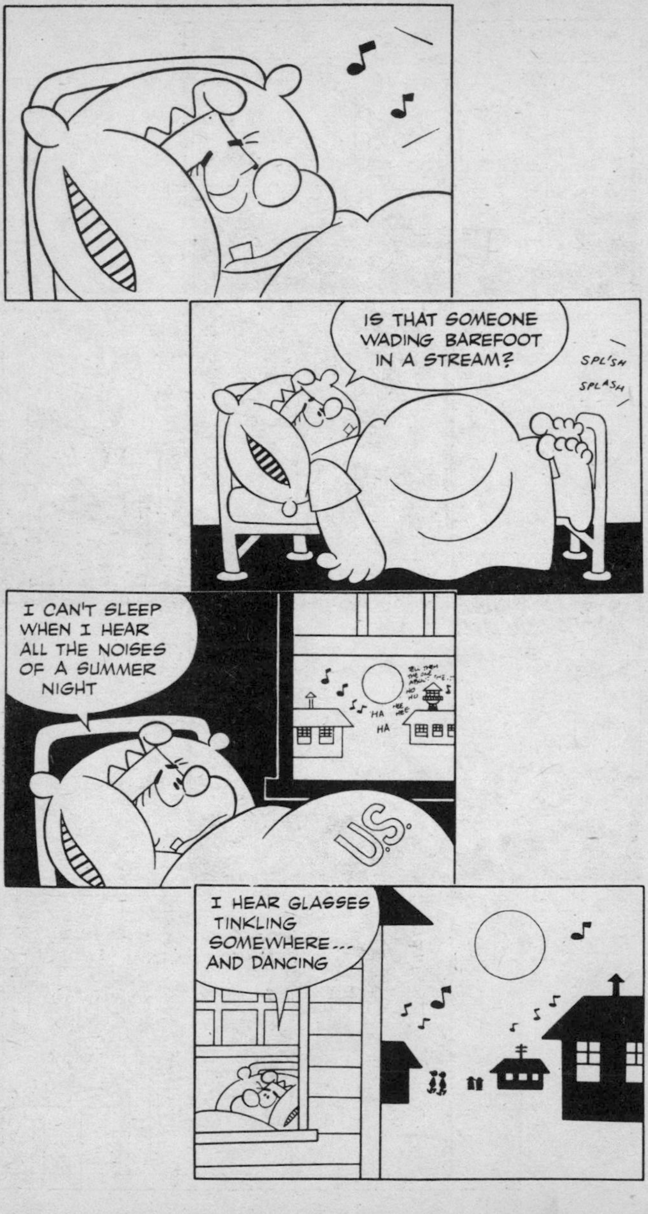
IS THAT SOMEONE WADING BAREFOOT IN A STREAM?
SPL'SH
SPLASH
I CAN'T SLEEP WHEN I HEAR ALL THE NOISES OF A SUMMER NIGHT
HA
HA
I HEAR GLASSES TINKLING SOMEWHERE... AND DANCING

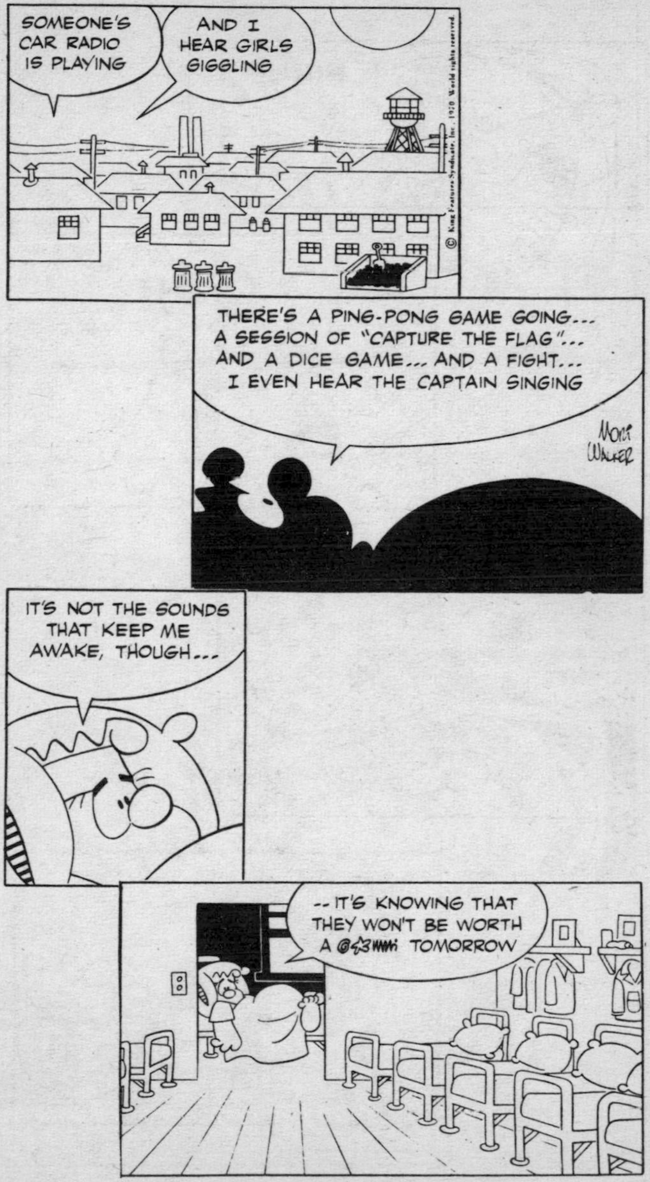
SOMEONE'S CAR RADIO IS PLAYING
AND I HEAR GIRLS GIGGLING
© King Features Syndicate, Inc., 1970 World rights reserved.
THERE'S A PING-PONG GAME GOING... A SESSION OF "CAPTURE THE FLAG"... AND A DICE GAME... AND A FIGHT... I EVEN HEAR THE CAPTAIN SINGING
MORT WALKER
IT'S NOT THE SOUNDS THAT KEEP ME AWAKE, THOUGH...
--IT'S KNOWING THAT THEY WON'T BE WORTH A @✱$!!! TOMORROW

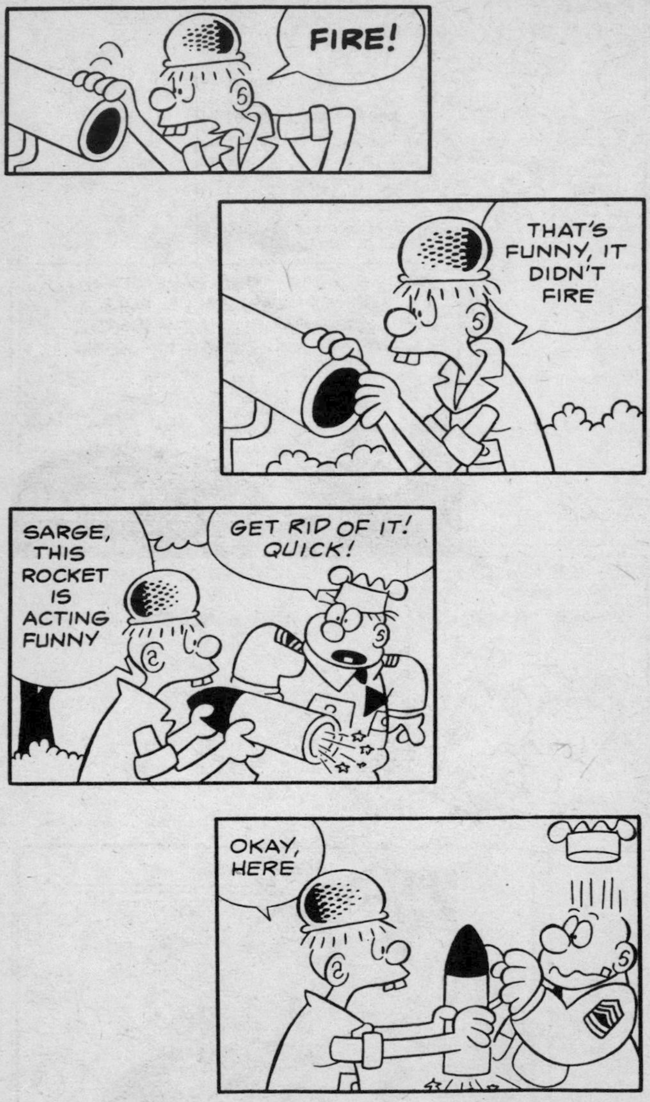
FIRE!
THAT'S FUNNY, IT DIDN'T FIRE
SARGE, THIS ROCKET IS ACTING FUNNY
GET RID OF IT! QUICK!
OKAY, HERE

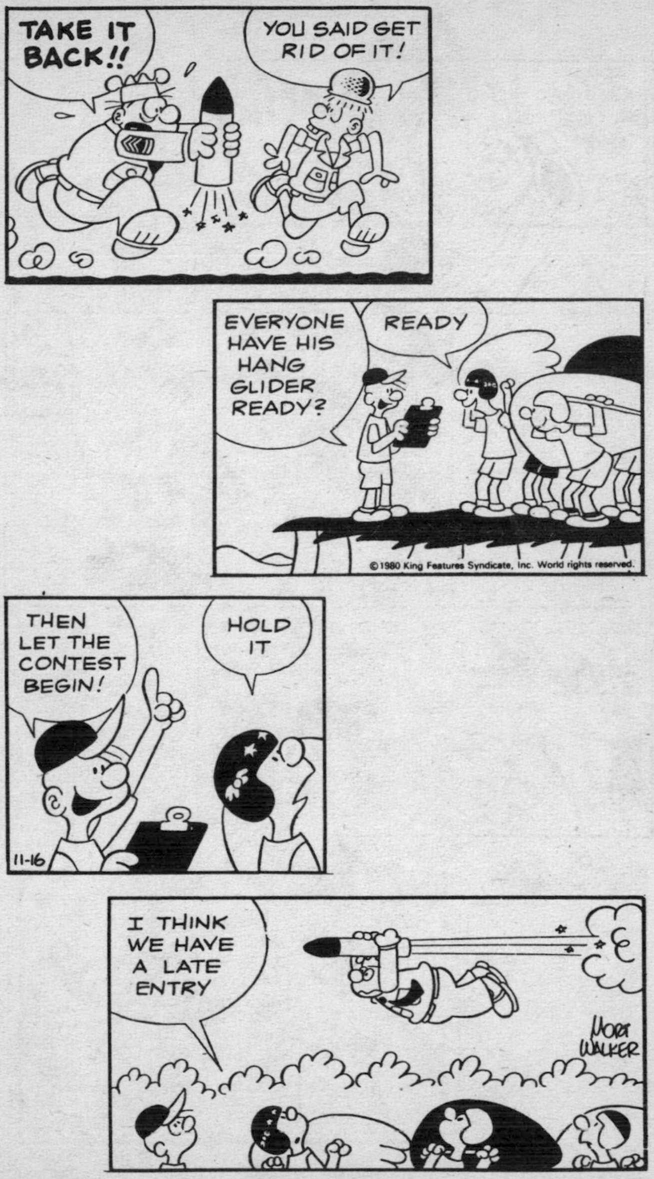
TAKE IT BACK!!
YOU SAID GET RID OF IT!
EVERYONE HAVE HIS HANG GLIDER READY?
READY
©1980 King Features Syndicate, Inc. World rights reserved.
THEN LET THE CONTEST BEGIN!
HOLD IT
11-16
I THINK WE HAVE A LATE ENTRY
MORT WALKER

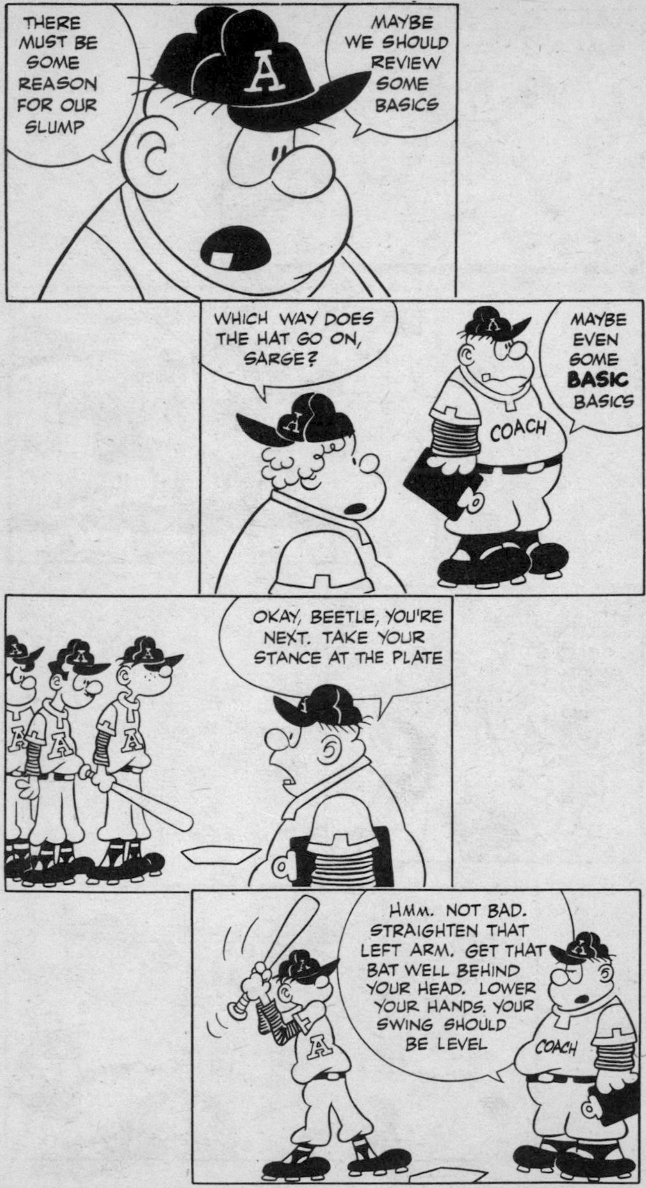
THERE MUST BE SOME REASON FOR OUR SLUMP
MAYBE WE SHOULD REVIEW SOME BASICS
WHICH WAY DOES THE HAT GO ON, SARGE?
MAYBE EVEN SOME **BASIC** BASICS
COACH
OKAY, BEETLE, YOU'RE NEXT. TAKE YOUR STANCE AT THE PLATE
HMM. NOT BAD. STRAIGHTEN THAT LEFT ARM. GET THAT BAT WELL BEHIND YOUR HEAD. LOWER YOUR HANDS. YOUR SWING SHOULD BE LEVEL
COACH

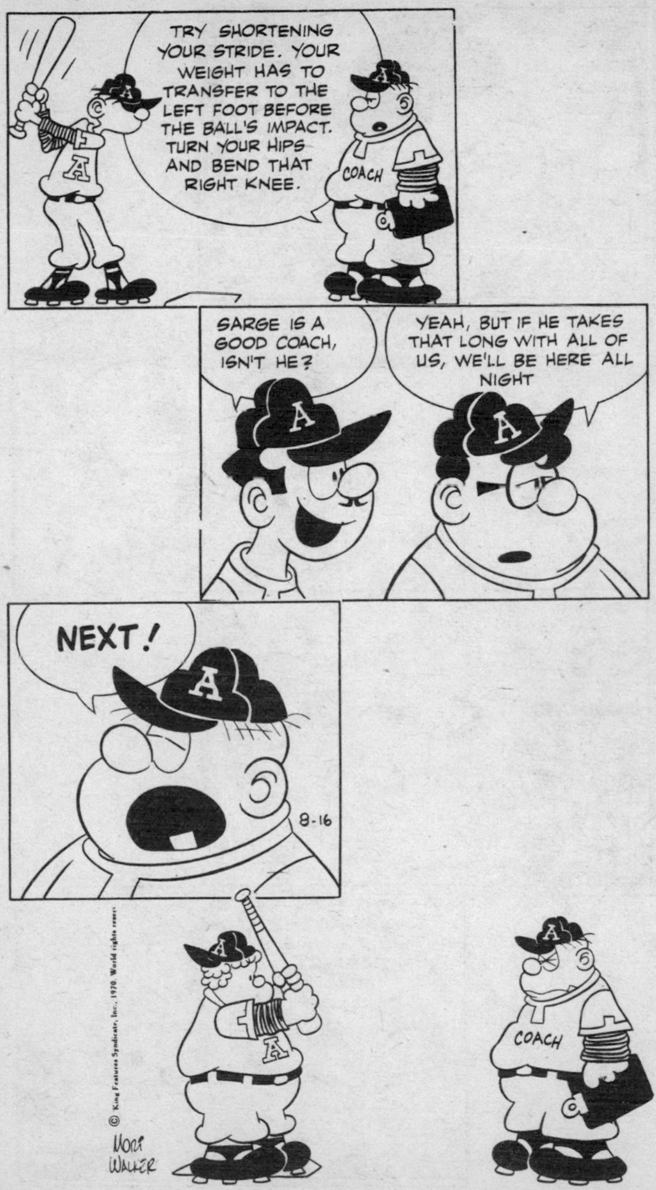

TRY SHORTENING YOUR STRIDE. YOUR WEIGHT HAS TO TRANSFER TO THE LEFT FOOT BEFORE THE BALL'S IMPACT. TURN YOUR HIPS AND BEND THAT RIGHT KNEE.
COACH
SARGE IS A GOOD COACH, ISN'T HE?
YEAH, BUT IF HE TAKES THAT LONG WITH ALL OF US, WE'LL BE HERE ALL NIGHT
NEXT!
8-16
© King Features Syndicate, Inc., 1970. World rights reser
MORT WALKER
COACH

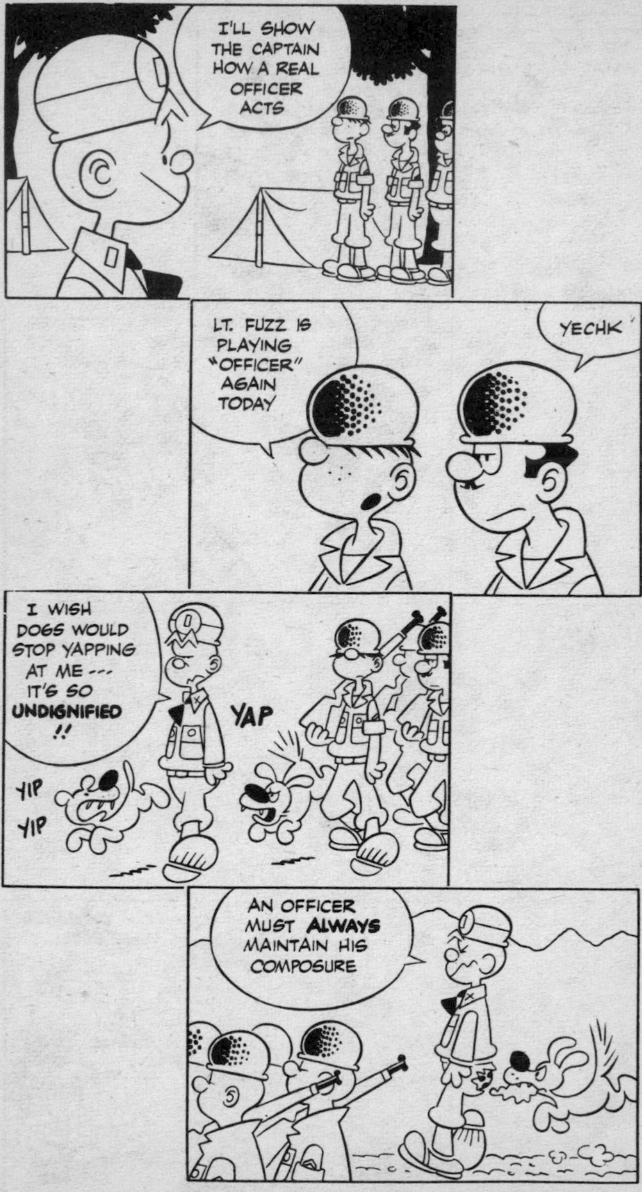
I'LL SHOW THE CAPTAIN HOW A REAL OFFICER ACTS
LT. FUZZ IS PLAYING "OFFICER" AGAIN TODAY
YECHK
I WISH DOGS WOULD STOP YAPPING AT ME --- IT'S SO **UNDIGNIFIED** !!
YAP
YIP
YIP
AN OFFICER MUST **ALWAYS** MAINTAIN HIS COMPOSURE

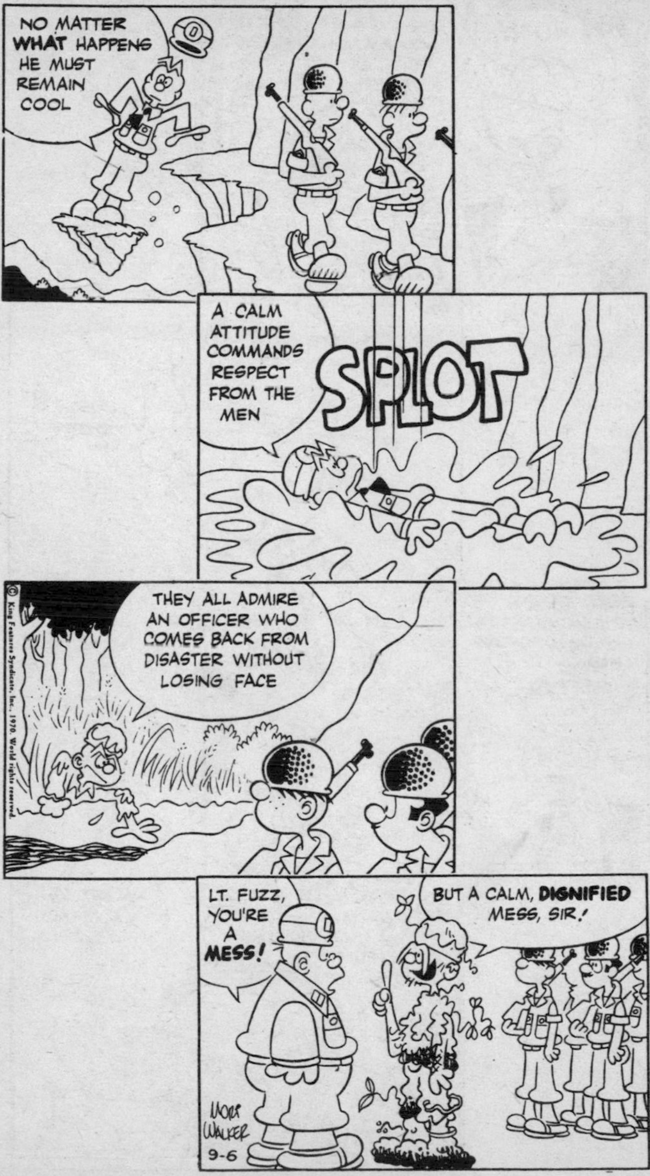
NO MATTER **WHAT** HAPPENS HE MUST REMAIN COOL
A CALM ATTITUDE COMMANDS RESPECT FROM THE MEN
SPLOT
THEY ALL ADMIRE AN OFFICER WHO COMES BACK FROM DISASTER WITHOUT LOSING FACE
© King Features Syndicate, Inc., 1970. World rights reserved.
LT. FUZZ, YOU'RE A **MESS!**
BUT A CALM, **DIGNIFIED** MESS, SIR!
MORT WALKER
9-6

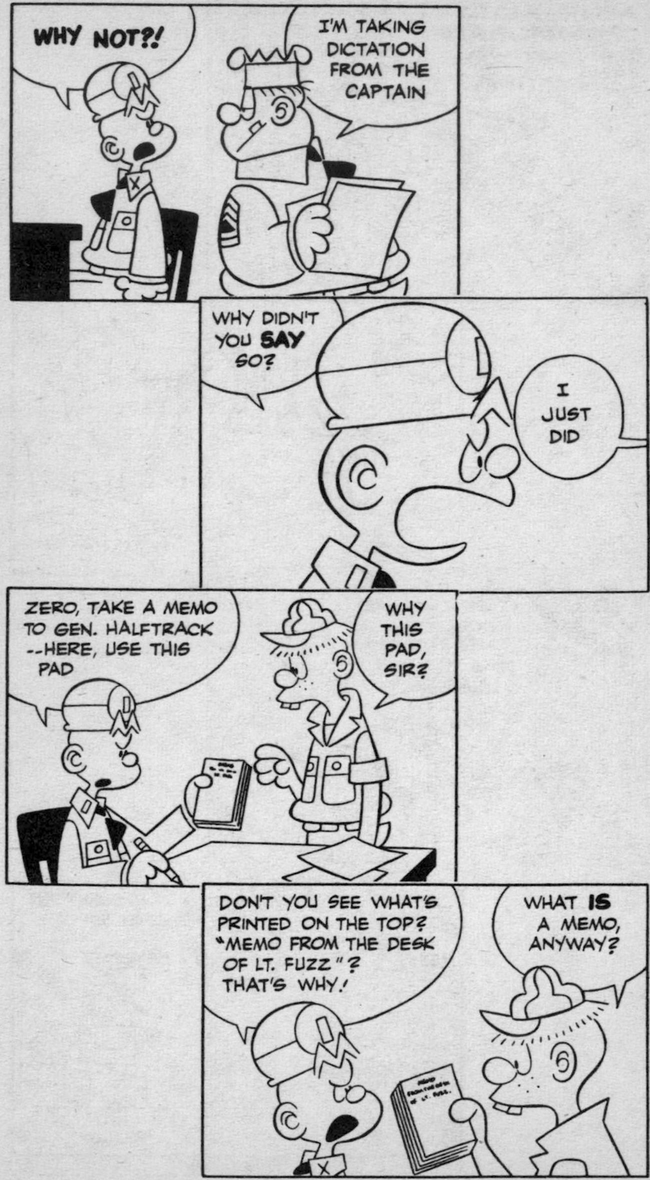
WHY NOT?!
I'M TAKING DICTATION FROM THE CAPTAIN
WHY DIDN'T YOU SAY SO?
I JUST DID
ZERO, TAKE A MEMO TO GEN. HALFTRACK --HERE, USE THIS PAD
WHY THIS PAD, SIR?
DON'T YOU SEE WHAT'S PRINTED ON THE TOP? "MEMO FROM THE DESK OF LT. FUZZ"? THAT'S WHY!
WHAT IS A MEMO, ANYWAY?

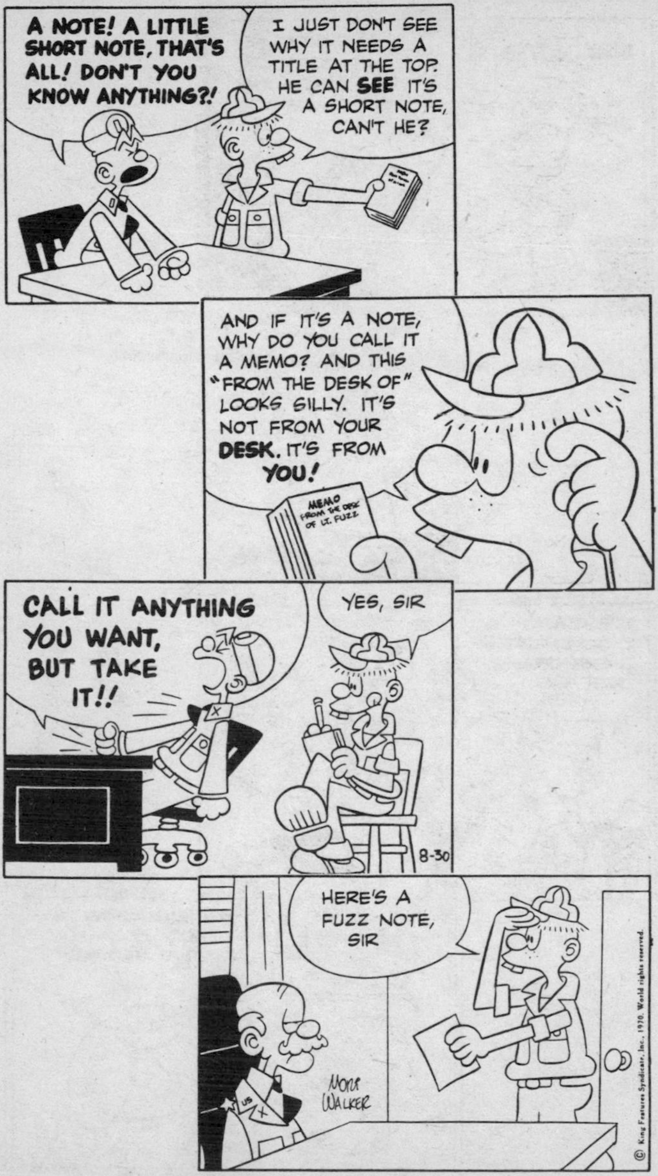
A NOTE! A LITTLE SHORT NOTE, THAT'S ALL! DON'T YOU KNOW ANYTHING?!
I JUST DON'T SEE WHY IT NEEDS A TITLE AT THE TOP. HE CAN SEE IT'S A SHORT NOTE, CAN'T HE?
AND IF IT'S A NOTE, WHY DO YOU CALL IT A MEMO? AND THIS "FROM THE DESK OF" LOOKS SILLY. IT'S NOT FROM YOUR DESK. IT'S FROM YOU!
MEMO FROM THE DESK OF LT. FUZZ
CALL IT ANYTHING YOU WANT, BUT TAKE IT!!
YES, SIR
8-30
HERE'S A FUZZ NOTE, SIR
MORT WALKER
© King Features Syndicate, Inc., 1970. World rights reserved.

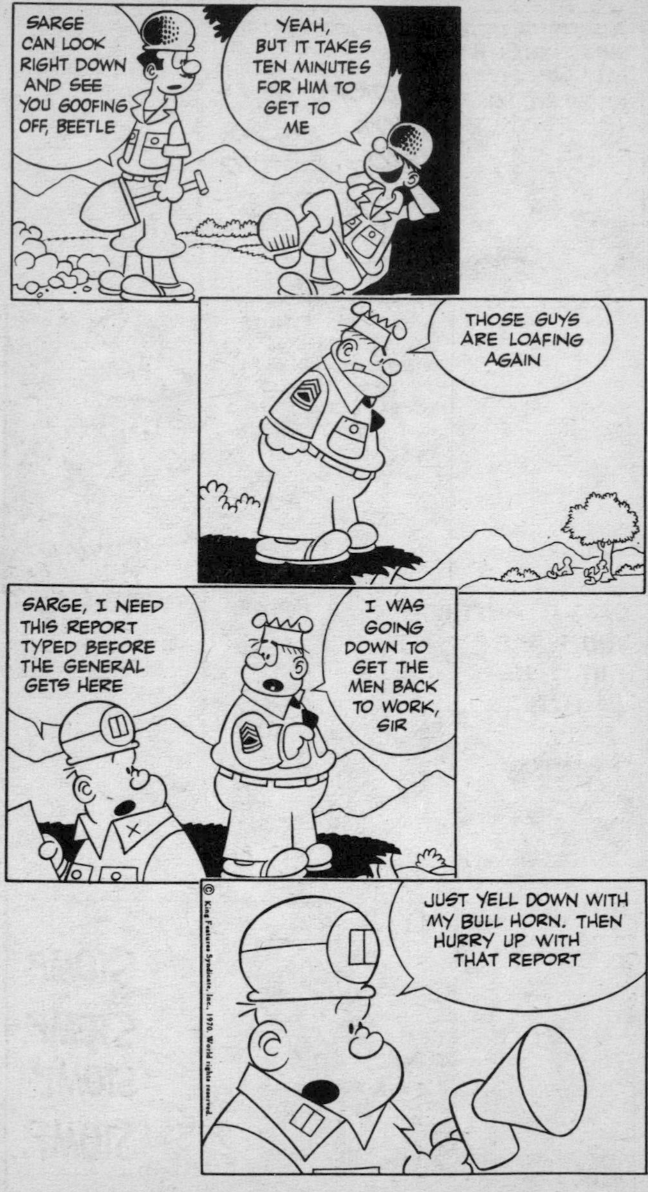
SARGE CAN LOOK RIGHT DOWN AND SEE YOU GOOFING OFF, BEETLE
YEAH, BUT IT TAKES TEN MINUTES FOR HIM TO GET TO ME
THOSE GUYS ARE LOAFING AGAIN
SARGE, I NEED THIS REPORT TYPED BEFORE THE GENERAL GETS HERE
I WAS GOING DOWN TO GET THE MEN BACK TO WORK, SIR
© King Features Syndicate, Inc., 1970. World rights reserved.
JUST YELL DOWN WITH MY BULL HORN. THEN HURRY UP WITH THAT REPORT

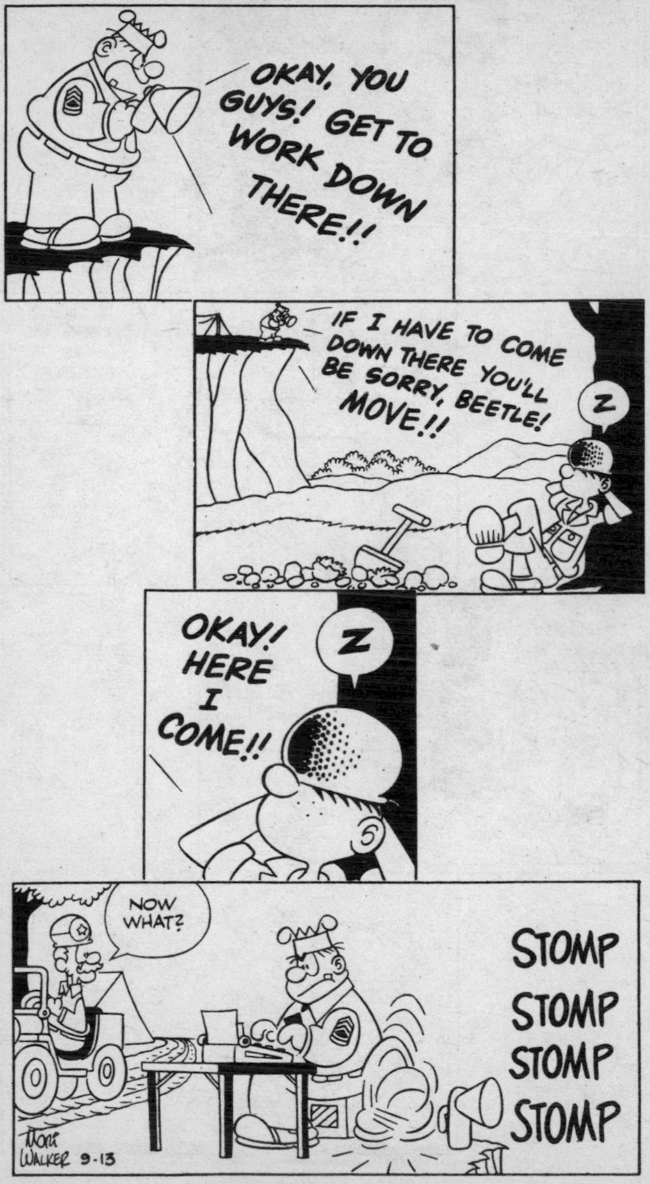
OKAY, YOU GUYS! GET TO WORK DOWN THERE!!
IF I HAVE TO COME DOWN THERE YOU'LL BE SORRY, BEETLE! MOVE!!
Z
OKAY! HERE I COME!!
Z
NOW WHAT?
STOMP
STOMP
STOMP
STOMP
MORT WALKER 9-13

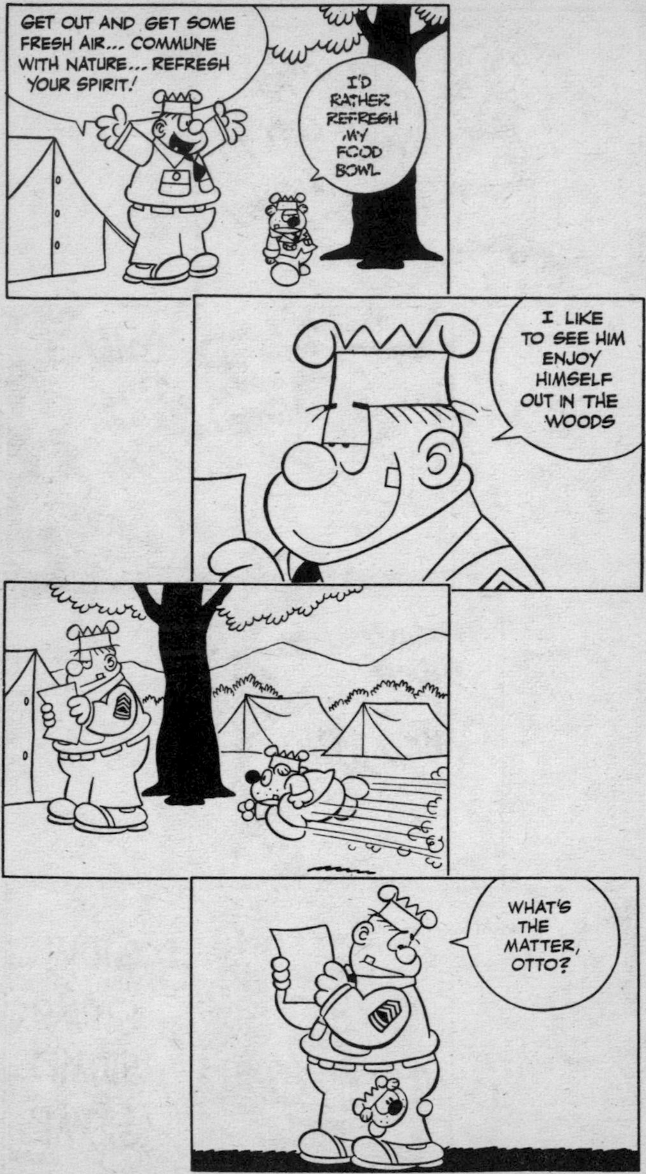
GET OUT AND GET SOME FRESH AIR... COMMUNE WITH NATURE... REFRESH YOUR SPIRIT!
I'D RATHER REFRESH MY FOOD BOWL
I LIKE TO SEE HIM ENJOY HIMSELF OUT IN THE WOODS
WHAT'S THE MATTER, OTTO?

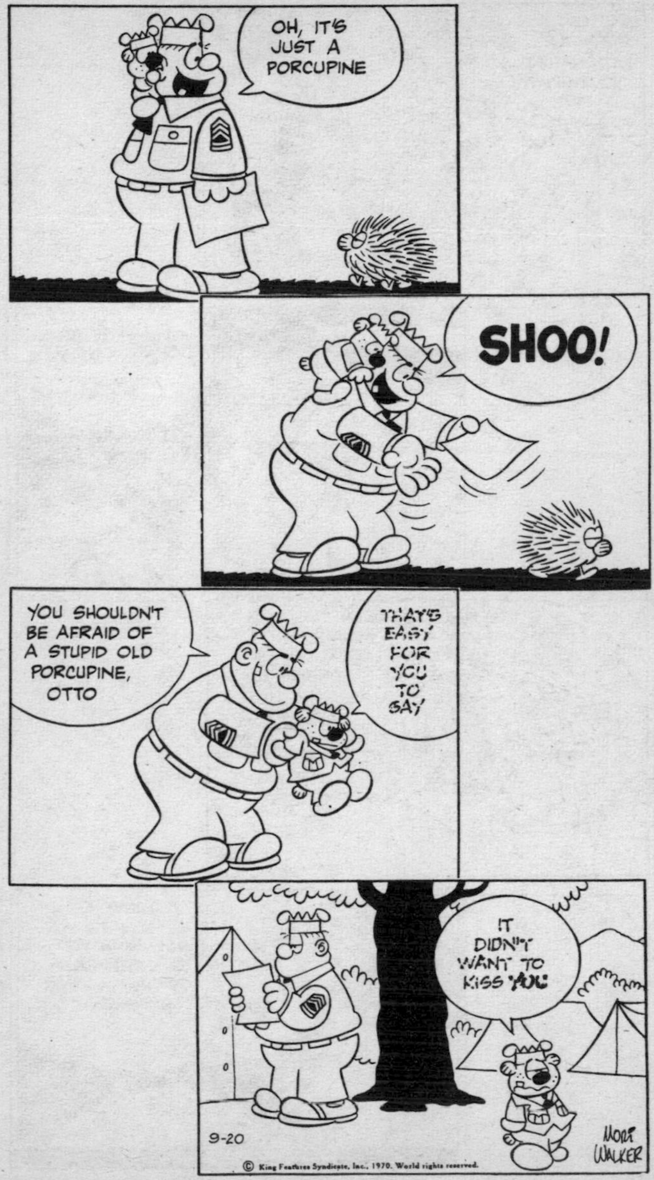
OH, IT'S JUST A PORCUPINE
SHOO!
YOU SHOULDN'T BE AFRAID OF A STUPID OLD PORCUPINE, OTTO
THAT'S EASY FOR YOU TO SAY
IT DIDN'T WANT TO KISS YOU
9-20
MORT WALKER
© King Features Syndicate, Inc., 1970. World rights reserved.

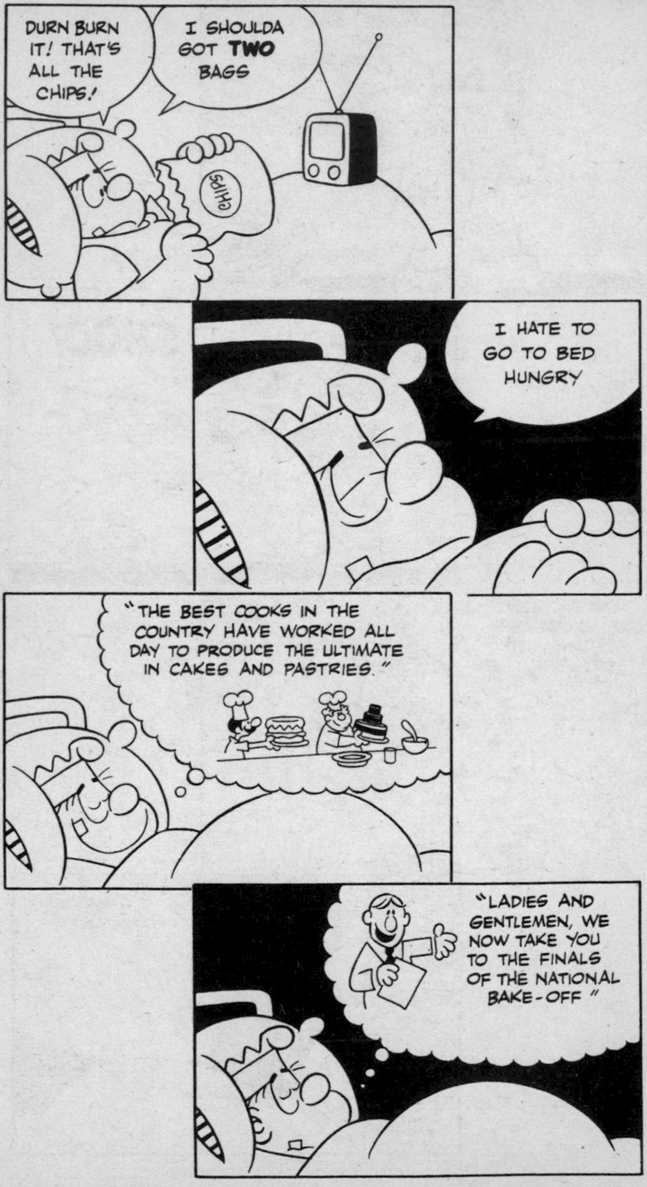
DURN BURN IT! THAT'S ALL THE CHIPS!
I SHOULDA GOT TWO BAGS
CHIPS
I HATE TO GO TO BED HUNGRY
"THE BEST COOKS IN THE COUNTRY HAVE WORKED ALL DAY TO PRODUCE THE ULTIMATE IN CAKES AND PASTRIES."
"LADIES AND GENTLEMEN, WE NOW TAKE YOU TO THE FINALS OF THE NATIONAL BAKE-OFF"

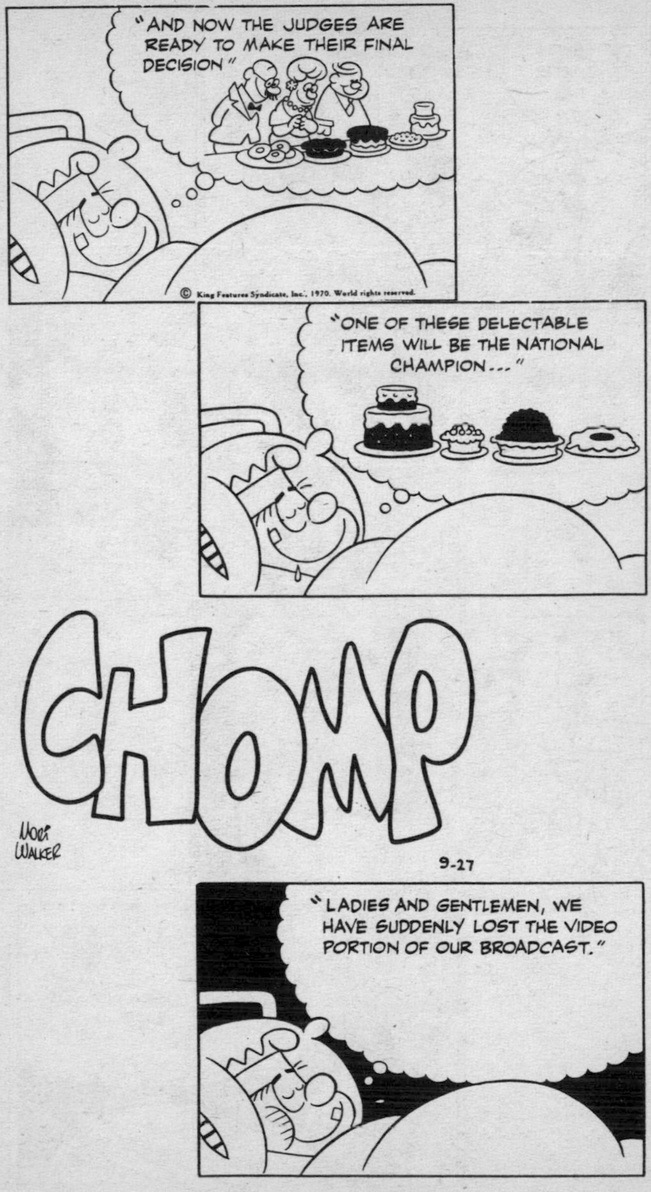
"AND NOW THE JUDGES ARE READY TO MAKE THEIR FINAL DECISION"
© King Features Syndicate, Inc., 1970. World rights reserved.
"ONE OF THESE DELECTABLE ITEMS WILL BE THE NATIONAL CHAMPION..."
CHOMP
MORT WALKER
9-27
"LADIES AND GENTLEMEN, WE HAVE SUDDENLY LOST THE VIDEO PORTION OF OUR BROADCAST."

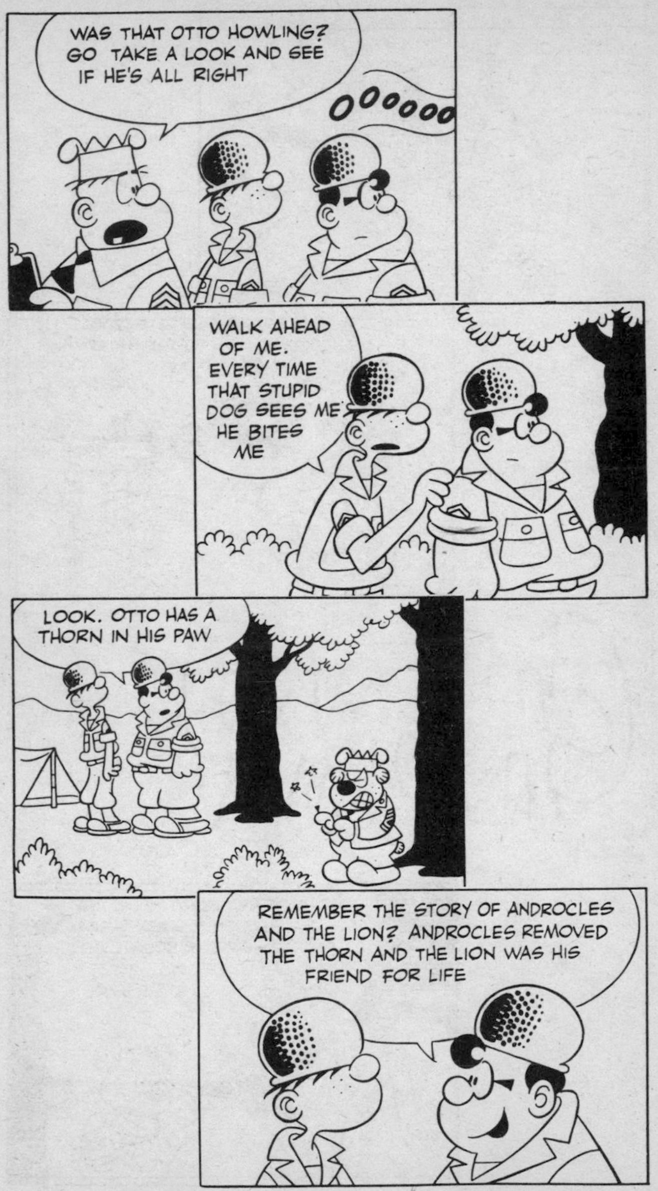
WAS THAT OTTO HOWLING? GO TAKE A LOOK AND SEE IF HE'S ALL RIGHT
OOOOOO
WALK AHEAD OF ME. EVERY TIME THAT STUPID DOG SEES ME HE BITES ME
LOOK. OTTO HAS A THORN IN HIS PAW
REMEMBER THE STORY OF ANDROCLES AND THE LION? ANDROCLES REMOVED THE THORN AND THE LION WAS HIS FRIEND FOR LIFE

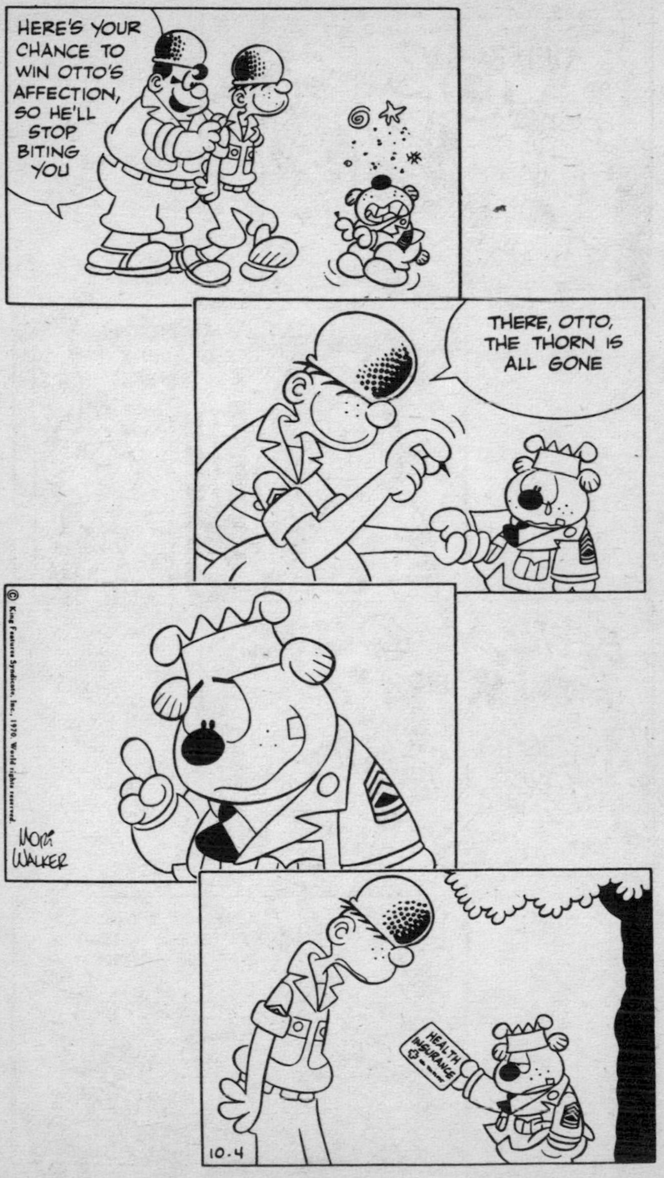
HERE'S YOUR CHANCE TO WIN OTTO'S AFFECTION, SO HE'LL STOP BITING YOU
THERE, OTTO, THE THORN IS ALL GONE
© King Features Syndicate, Inc., 1970. World rights reserved.
MORT WALKER
HEALTH INSURANCE
10-4

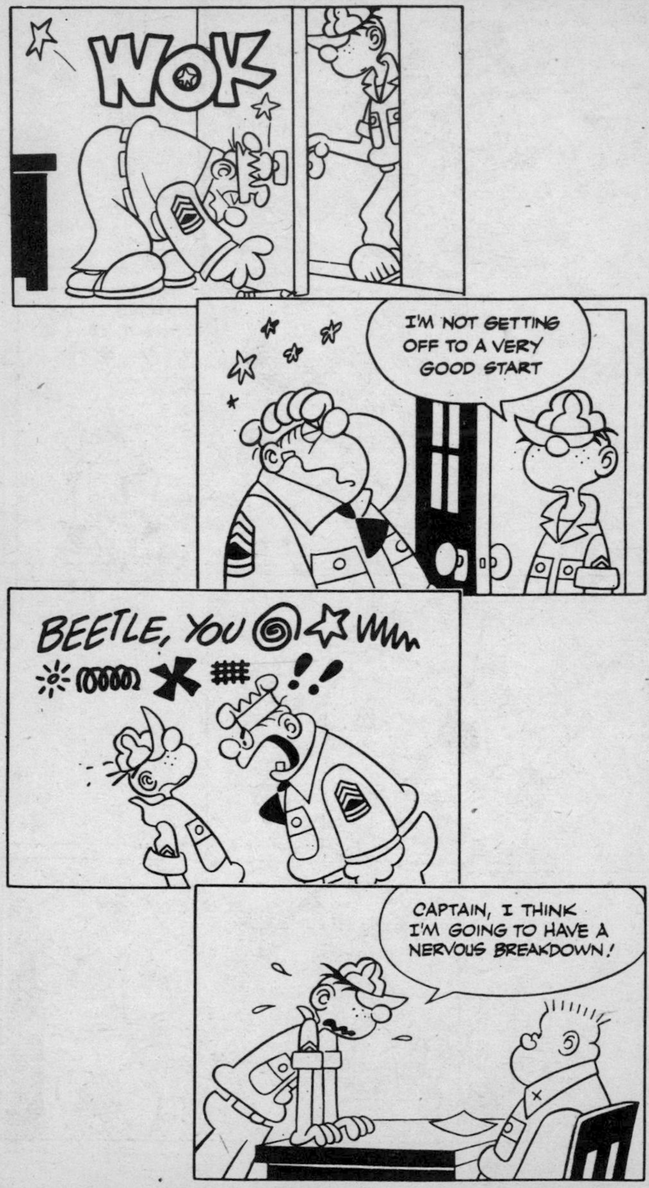
WOK
I'M NOT GETTING OFF TO A VERY GOOD START
BEETLE, YOU
CAPTAIN, I THINK I'M GOING TO HAVE A NERVOUS BREAKDOWN!

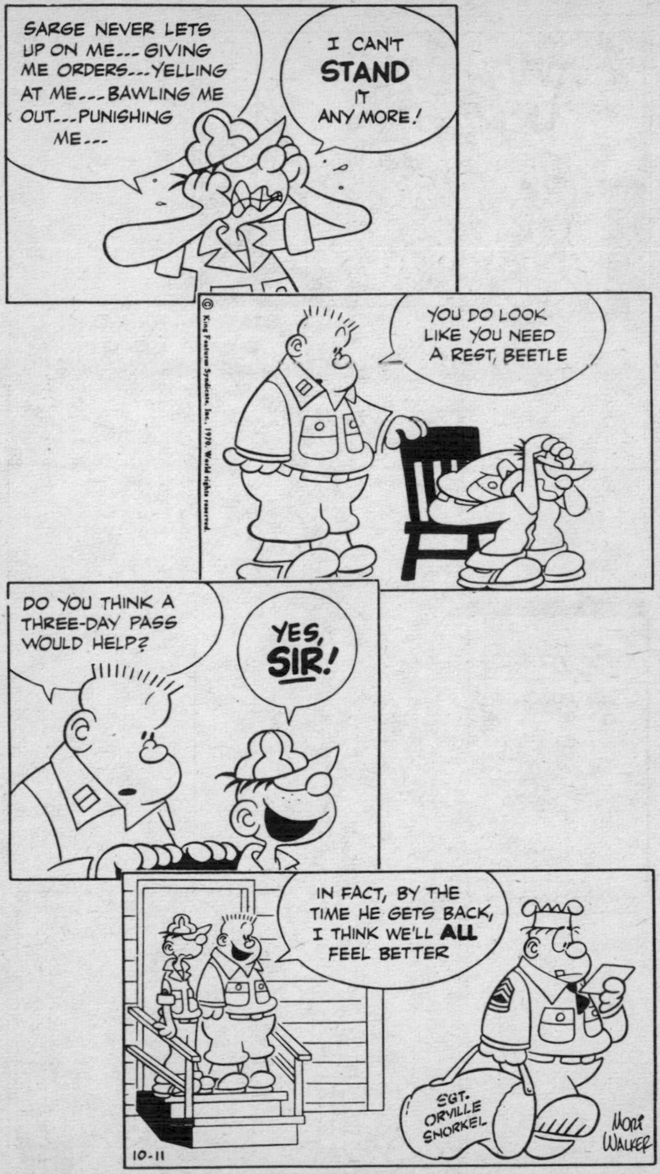
SARGE NEVER LETS UP ON ME--- GIVING ME ORDERS---YELLING AT ME---BAWLING ME OUT---PUNISHING ME---
I CAN'T STAND IT ANY MORE!
© King Features Syndicate, Inc., 1970. World rights reserved.
YOU DO LOOK LIKE YOU NEED A REST, BEETLE
DO YOU THINK A THREE-DAY PASS WOULD HELP?
YES, SIR!
IN FACT, BY THE TIME HE GETS BACK, I THINK WE'LL ALL FEEL BETTER
SGT. ORVILLE SNORKEL
MORT WALKER
10-11

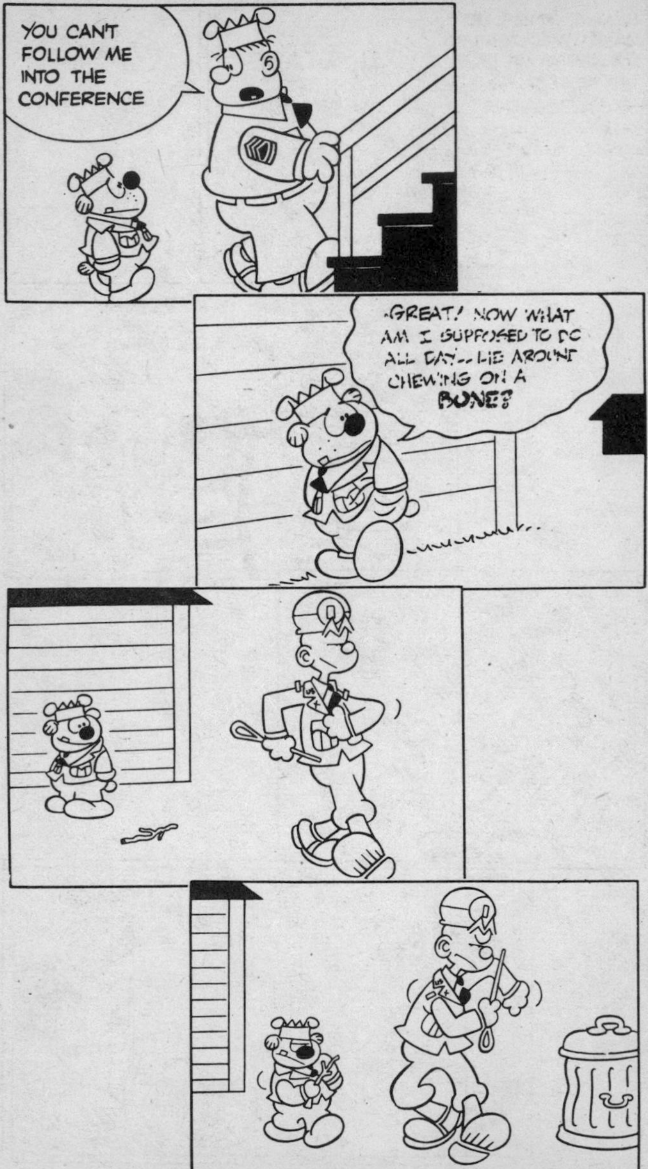
YOU CAN'T FOLLOW ME INTO THE CONFERENCE
GREAT! NOW WHAT AM I SUPPOSED TO DO ALL DAY-- LIE AROUND CHEWING ON A BONE?

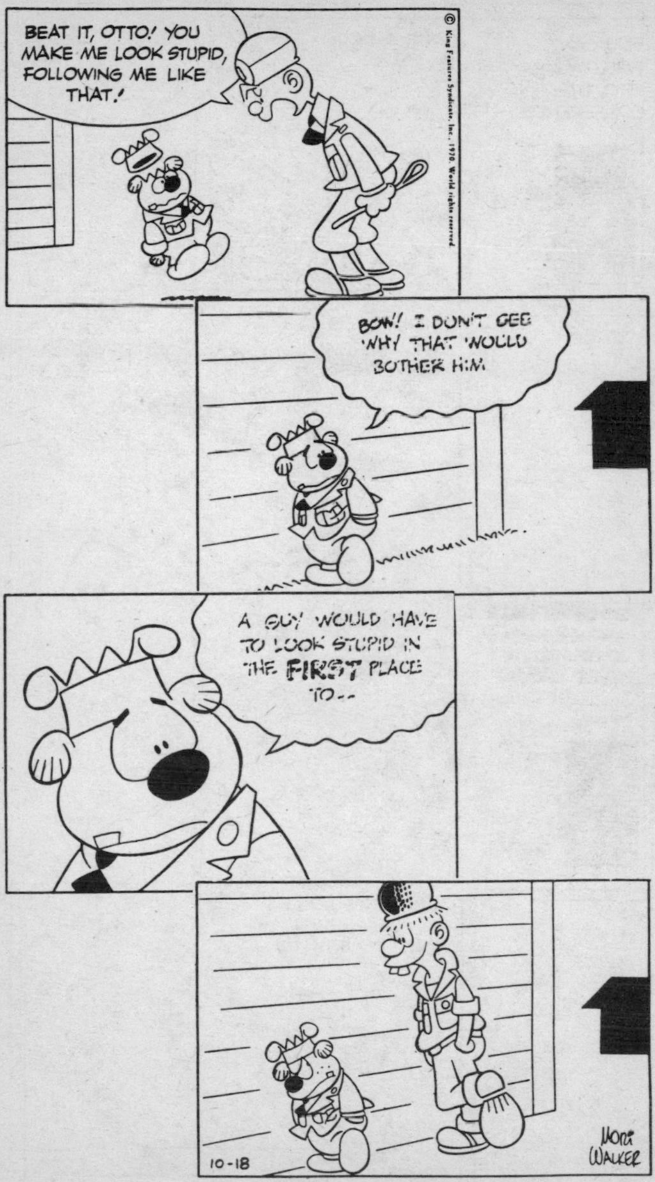
BEAT IT, OTTO! YOU MAKE ME LOOK STUPID, FOLLOWING ME LIKE THAT!
© King Features Syndicate, Inc., 1970. World rights reserved.
BOW! I DON'T SEE WHY THAT WOULD BOTHER HIM
A GUY WOULD HAVE TO LOOK STUPID IN THE FIRST PLACE TO--
10-18
MORT WALKER

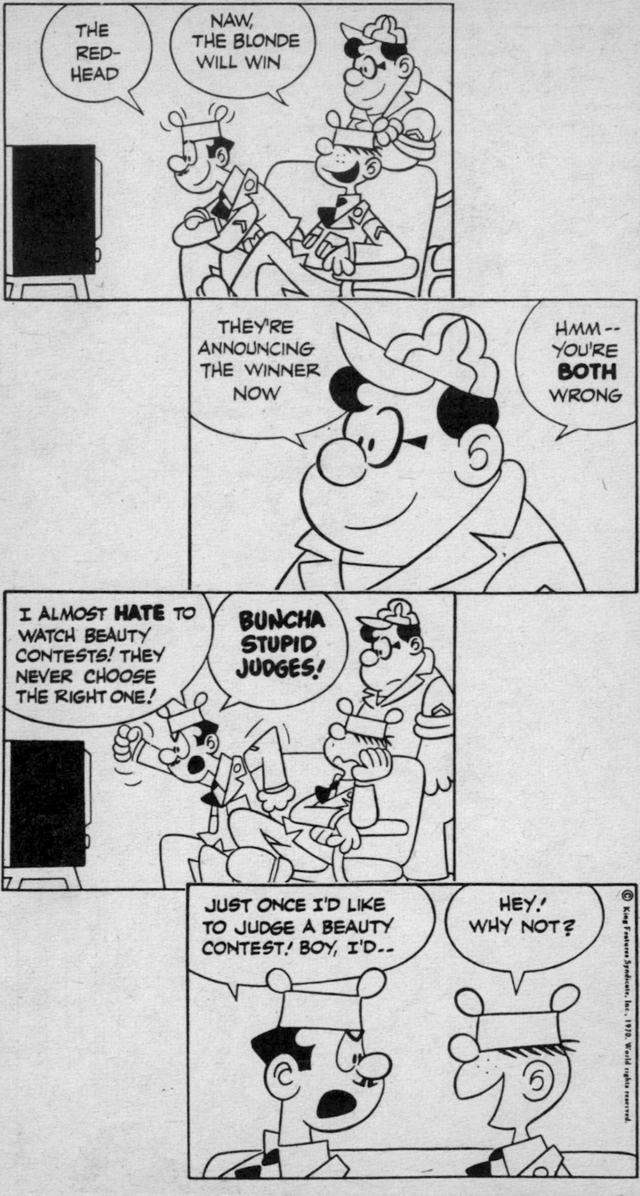
THE RED-HEAD
NAW, THE BLONDE WILL WIN
THEY'RE ANNOUNCING THE WINNER NOW
HMM-- YOU'RE BOTH WRONG
I ALMOST HATE TO WATCH BEAUTY CONTESTS! THEY NEVER CHOOSE THE RIGHT ONE!
BUNCHA STUPID JUDGES!
JUST ONCE I'D LIKE TO JUDGE A BEAUTY CONTEST! BOY, I'D--
HEY! WHY NOT?
© King Features Syndicate, Inc. 1970. World rights reserved.

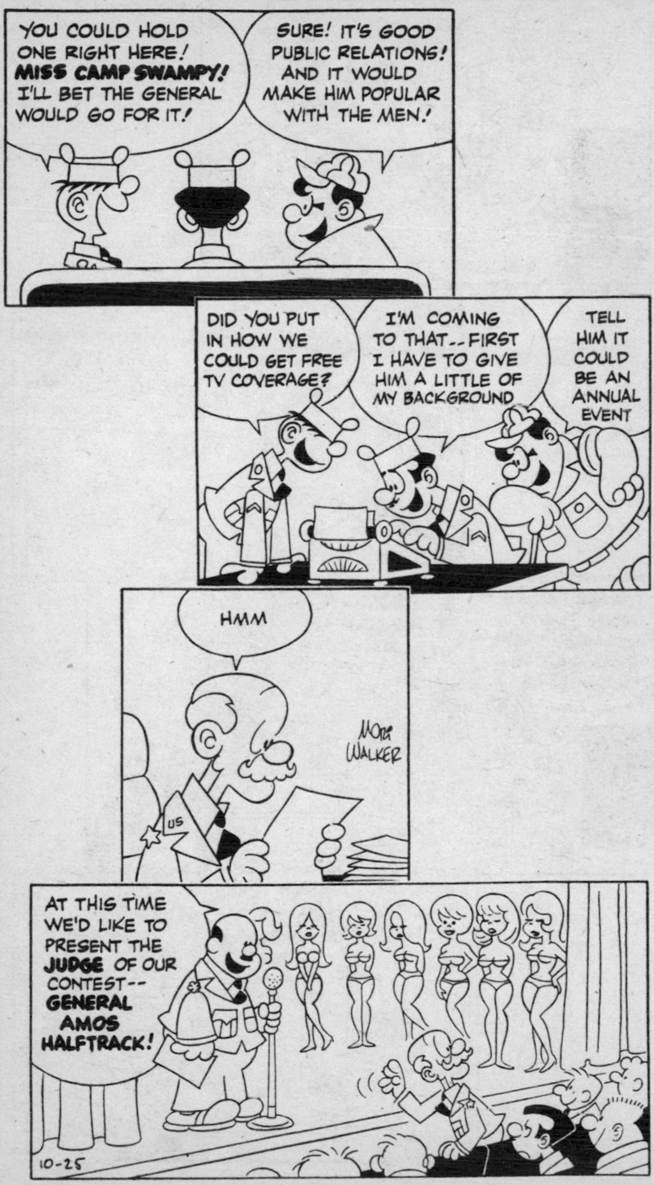
YOU COULD HOLD ONE RIGHT HERE! **MISS CAMP SWAMPY!** I'LL BET THE GENERAL WOULD GO FOR IT!
SURE! IT'S GOOD PUBLIC RELATIONS! AND IT WOULD MAKE HIM POPULAR WITH THE MEN!
DID YOU PUT IN HOW WE COULD GET FREE TV COVERAGE?
I'M COMING TO THAT-- FIRST I HAVE TO GIVE HIM A LITTLE OF MY BACKGROUND
TELL HIM IT COULD BE AN ANNUAL EVENT
HMM
MORT WALKER
US
AT THIS TIME WE'D LIKE TO PRESENT THE **JUDGE** OF OUR CONTEST-- **GENERAL AMOS HALFTRACK!**
10-25

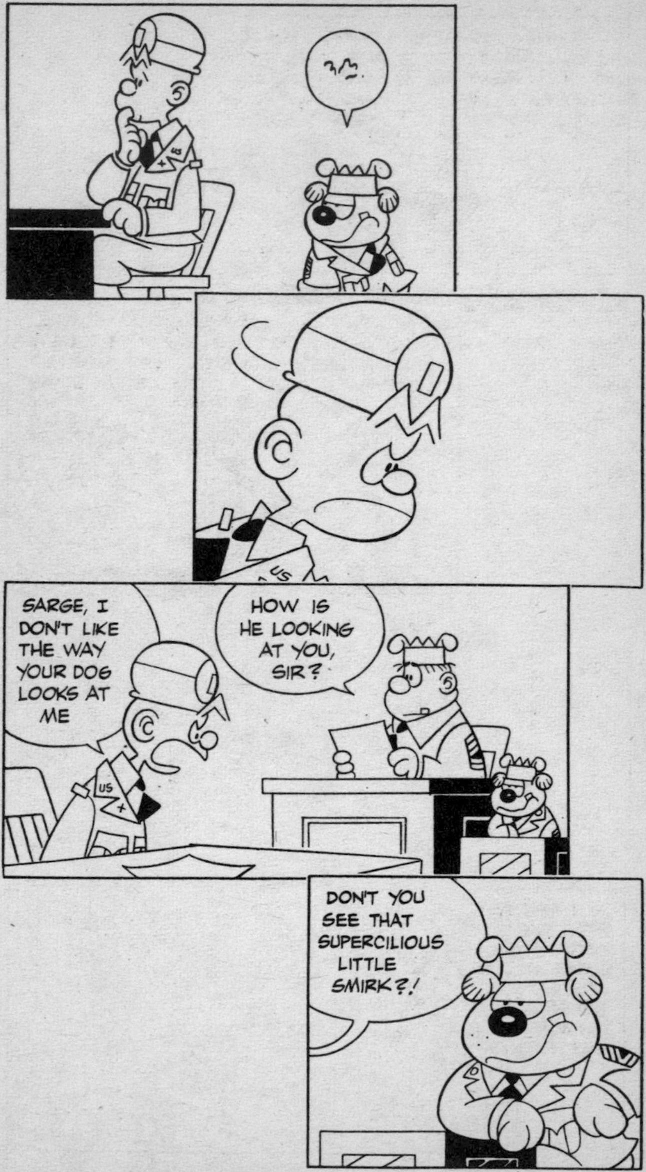

SARGE, I DON'T LIKE THE WAY YOUR DOG LOOKS AT ME
HOW IS HE LOOKING AT YOU, SIR?
DON'T YOU SEE THAT SUPERCILIOUS LITTLE SMIRK?!

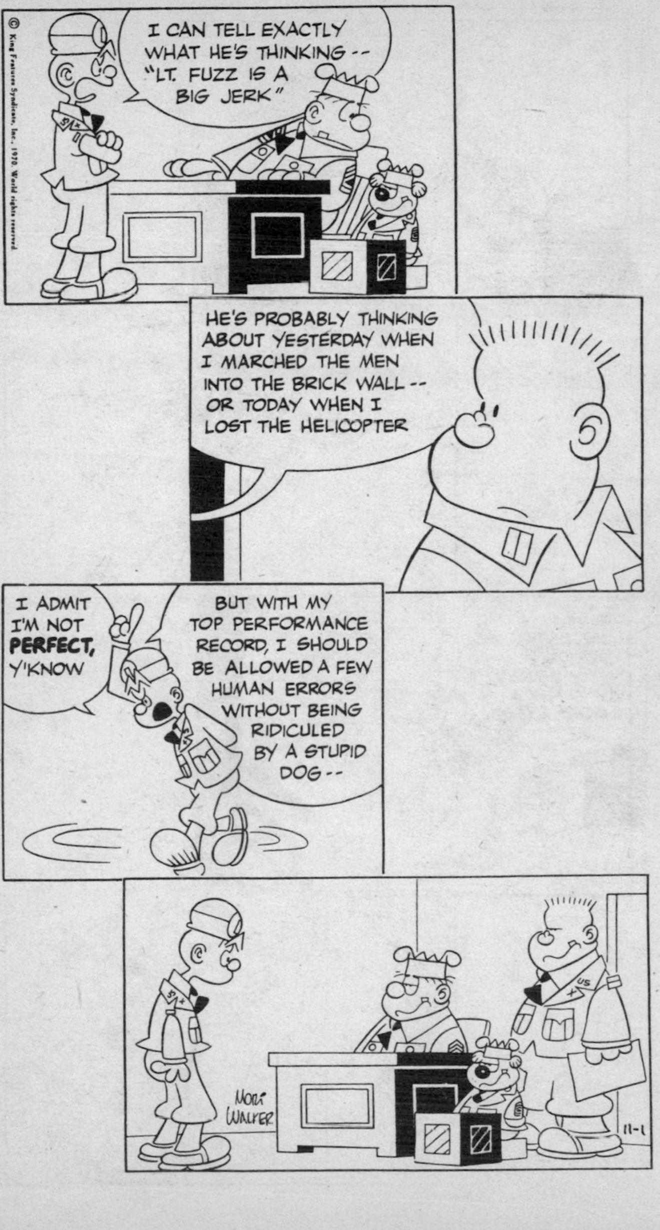
© King Features Syndicate, Inc., 1970. World rights reserved.
I CAN TELL EXACTLY WHAT HE'S THINKING -- "LT. FUZZ IS A BIG JERK"
HE'S PROBABLY THINKING ABOUT YESTERDAY WHEN I MARCHED THE MEN INTO THE BRICK WALL -- OR TODAY WHEN I LOST THE HELICOPTER
I ADMIT I'M NOT **PERFECT,** Y'KNOW
BUT WITH MY TOP PERFORMANCE RECORD, I SHOULD BE ALLOWED A FEW HUMAN ERRORS WITHOUT BEING RIDICULED BY A STUPID DOG --
US
MORT WALKER
11-1

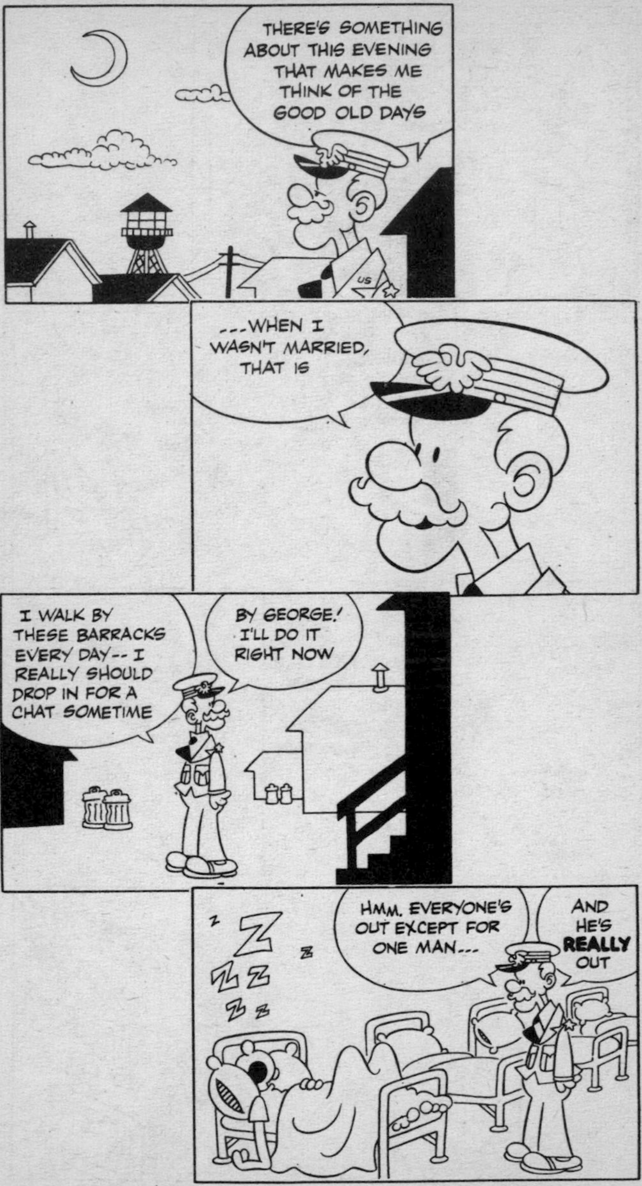
THERE'S SOMETHING ABOUT THIS EVENING THAT MAKES ME THINK OF THE GOOD OLD DAYS
US
---WHEN I WASN'T MARRIED, THAT IS
I WALK BY THESE BARRACKS EVERY DAY-- I REALLY SHOULD DROP IN FOR A CHAT SOMETIME
BY GEORGE! I'LL DO IT RIGHT NOW
Z Z Z Z Z Z Z Z
HMM. EVERYONE'S OUT EXCEPT FOR ONE MAN---
AND HE'S **REALLY** OUT

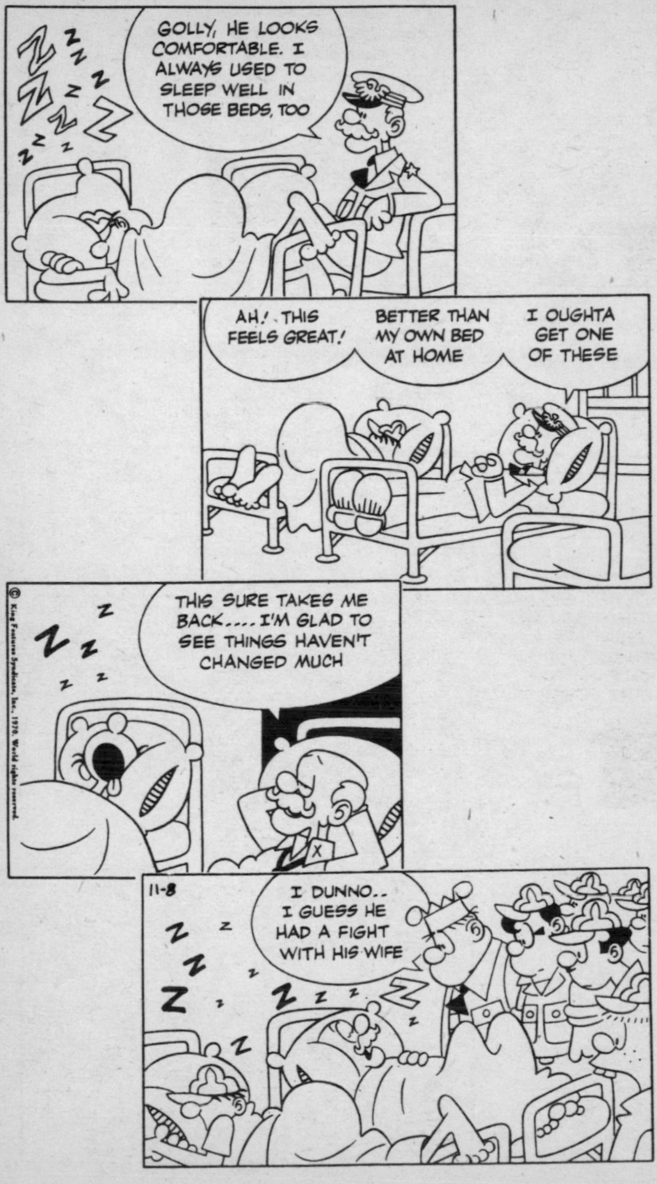

GOLLY, HE LOOKS COMFORTABLE. I ALWAYS USED TO SLEEP WELL IN THOSE BEDS, TOO
AH! THIS FEELS GREAT!
BETTER THAN MY OWN BED AT HOME
I OUGHTA GET ONE OF THESE
© King Features Syndicate, Inc., 1970. World rights reserved.
THIS SURE TAKES ME BACK.... I'M GLAD TO SEE THINGS HAVEN'T CHANGED MUCH
11-8
I DUNNO.. I GUESS HE HAD A FIGHT WITH HIS WIFE